MEMOIRS

OF A WEDDING DJ

MEMOIRS
OF A WEDDING DJ

by

Brent Faddies

Written by Brent Faddies

www.djbfad.com

ISBN: 978-1-7772579-2-7

Disclaimer:

Some names and identifying details have been changed to protect the privacy of individuals.

I have tried to recreate events, locales, and conversations from my memories of them. In order to maintain their anonymity in some instances I have changed the names of individuals and places. I may have changed some identifying characteristics and details such as physical properties, occupations, and places of residence.

(Memoir, Autobiography)

This book is a memoir. It reflects the author's present recollections of experiences over time. Some names and characteristics have been changed, some events have been compressed, and some dialogue has been recreated.

Dedicated to all the crazies

who continue to choose and celebrate love!

CONTENTS

LAST CALL

PROLOGUE

CHICKEN DANCE

July 2012

The sister-of-the-bride uttered the four words no DJ wants to hear.

"'Chicken Dance.' We're ready!"

She's smiling, but her voice is sharp and impatient. The family is gathering behind her, and someone is helping Grandma up from her chair.

I do a double-take.

"You mean, the actual 'Chicken Dance?' Na-na-na-na-na-na-na?" I laugh and sing it for reference while doing the arm-clucking movements.

"That's it, next song!" she says.

I raise my eyebrows, "You're serious?"

"Yes!" she snaps. "Didn't my sister tell you? My family does it at every wedding!"

Thoughts flash through my head.

One: This must be a joke. Two: Did the bride actually tell me to play the "Chicken Dance?" And most importantly, three: I don't have the "Chicken Dance . . ."

This was supposed to be the dictionary definition of a low-maintenance wedding.

As a client referral, the bride booked online and paid the full amount in advance. There were no cheesy song requests . . . no requests at all, actually.

"Just play good music," she had written in her last email.

I knew something was going to go wrong tonight.

The parking lot was already half full of convertibles and pickup trucks when I arrived. A rag-tag group of at least 60 people was already going hard, passing spliffs, and taking swigs from small bottles of vodka. I park beside a pickup truck with Calgary plates and a bumper sticker that says I'm Swervin' Cuz I'm Pervin'. It was obvious that most of these people were starting the celebration earlier . . . much earlier.

Inside the community hall, I begin my setup on the stage at the back of the room. The bride had told me there would be about 100 guests. The guest list must have swelled significantly as I showed up to a sea of tables and place settings for over 300.

The bar was to the left of the stage, the toilets to the right—a serious design flaw. Throughout the night, there would be a constant lineup for both, along with the smell of vomit and hair spray hanging like a thick blanket over the DJ booth throughout the night.

Now I need to figure out if I even have the "Chicken Dance" song!

I do a quick search of my music files and come up blank. My mouth is dry, and my head starts to spin.

"Nobody told me . . ." I start in, but the sister-of-the-bride is having none of it.

"Everyone's ready, next song!" she repeats, visibly annoyed. Then she spins and walks toward the crowd on the dance floor.

I tell myself to stay calm, but my brain is fluttering, trying to think of a solution. Try as I might, there's no getting past the glaringly obvious point that I don't have the "Chicken Dance." And the reason I don't have the "Chicken Dance" is because I've never played it! I have prided myself in never having played it, on never being that DJ who resorts to such cheap tactics. But tonight, as it turns out, my reputation (and job) depends on it.

I remember in the 80s, the "Chicken Dance" was played at every wedding I went to as a kid, almost like an obligation. I would never imagine having it in my catalog, but right now, I'd be happy to just press play and get this over with.

The song playing starts fading out. Don't panic, I tell myself; I've got about 20 seconds. Instinctively, I cue up another song just in case this is actually a nightmare I'm about to wake up from. Meanwhile, I rescan my songs for the "Chicken Dance," but it's completely pointless. I don't have it.

The sister-of-the-bride's patience is long gone. Behind her, the family members have gathered into a sea of pinstripe shirts and spiked hair.

Some guy is whirling his belt around like a lasso, and another has a tie around his forehead.

I see Grandma wobbling her way over to the dance floor, resting a hand on her cane. She's a dead ringer for Anne Ramsey, that grumpy lady in the 80s comedy, Throw Mama from the Train. She picks her spot on the floor directly in front of me and passes her cane to an uncle, then starts pumping her fist in anticipation while the crowd hollers in approval—and why not! This is evidently her big moment.

I mutter under my breath, "Why wouldn't the bride tell me this is her family's wedding song?" I feel my nervousness changing to frustration, then to anger. "What kind of stupid idiot bride doesn't tell her DJ about the family's big song?"

It's too late to dwell on past misunderstandings. And besides, in about a minute, they are absolutely going to lose their minds when they find out I don't have their song.

I pull out my phone, praying the venue has a strong enough Wi-Fi signal. It's a community hall just off the highway, and my connection has been patchy all night. My browser opens, and the internet connection stalls. Seconds tick past like hours.

Finally! I open YouTube and frantically type "CHICKEN DANCE" into the search box. Small thumbnails of "Chicken Dances" pop up on the screen. I scroll through them, scrutinizing the options: live recordings in school gyms, Bavarian beer halls, kid's TV shows. Then, a computer-generated cartoon chicken! It's the most legitimate-looking version; it has the most views. I check the play length: 2:43. I inhale, pray, and click it.

By now, the previous song has faded out, replaced by dead silence. I swallow, watching the little line move across the screen: Buffering 28%. I need to fill some time while the video loads. Say something!

Picking up the microphone, I force myself to speak.

"Hi, everyone." It echoes slightly, too loud for the quiet space. The crowd quietens down, and I feel a flush of embarrassment but hold my composure. My eyes watch the red buffering line slowly stretch across the screen.

"We have a special song coming up!" I try to sound excited, but it comes out flat. I hear someone cough. Another clinks a glass. The awkward silence of 300 people staring at me is unbearable. "Can I get everyone on the dance floor?" I make a big show of waving them over, a blatant ploy to buy more time.

"Trust me," I say. "This will be worth it . . ."

With my hand shaking, I pull down the main volume slider, then yank out the plug from the mixer and insert it into the phone's headphone jack.

Why wasn't I more prepared? A wave of self-loathing comes over me as I watch the line creep across the screen. Buffering 78%. What the hell is with this slow Wi-Fi?

The two sides of my personality start dueling it out. The critical side screams, Every wedding DJ needs to have the "Chicken Dance!" My defensive side hits back, I didn't start DJing weddings to play the fucking "Chicken Dance!" I feel anger welling up inside my throat.

I'm not a wedding DJ! I yell inside my head. I never wanted this!

The red bar glows, and I take a deep breath. “Okay, everyone!” I bellow into the microphone. “Let’s hear it again for the bride and groom . . .” There are a few scattered claps and even more swaying bodies.

“Fuck-yeah!” one guy yells. “Let’s do this!”

My palms are sweaty, the phone slippery in my hand. I say a “Hail Mary” under my breath and hit play.

The accordion intro kicks in . . .

You may be asking yourself, as I often do, how did I end up here? DJing people’s weddings isn’t anything someone really aspires to; it’s more something you fall into. Believe me, I’ve asked myself that question plenty of times over the years. If you want a better answer than that, then I need to start the story much further back.

FIRST DANCE

CHAPTER 1

FIRED

July 17th, 2009

A message pops up on my computer screen.

1:00pm meeting with Vince [Accept: Yes/No]

I quickly close the browser window to the music site I had open, alongside the CRM program I was supposed to be working on. Then I quickly check over my shoulder to see if anyone noticed.

Strange, I thought the boss was out of town. With my hand on the mouse, I hover the pointer over the message. *It must be a conference call,* I think to myself.

Things have been different lately at my company XIZ. We were acquired recently by a larger German corporation, and the fact that we were doing pretty much the same jobs as our European counterparts wasn't making for good conversation around the water cooler. Layoffs had begun, and gossip swirled around the office about who would be next on the chopping block. As far as I was concerned, I was safe. My job in Sales Support was revenue-generating for the company. I take a deep breath, click *Accept,* then roll my chair back and take a large gulp of my Starbucks coffee.

I open the company's internal instant messaging system and type a message to the boss.

Hi Vince, how was Toronto?

Great. Did you get the meeting request I just sent?

Yes, I didn't know you were back in town.

Got back this morning.

Anything I need to prepare for?

No.

Okay. Just to let you know, I was ten minutes late today. I'll take it off my lunch.

No problem. See you at 1:00pm.

I take a swig of coffee, then stand up, popping my head over the cubicle beside me.

"Hey Jessica, did you get a meeting request from Vince?"

"Nope. You?" She says as she turns in her chair to face me.

"Yeah, 1:00pm," I answer back. "Strange . . ."

"Maybe he just needs to have the monthly report early," she says. "By the way, where're you going for lunch?"

I step out into the sunshine, walk toward Coopers' Park on Vancouver's False Creek waterfront. I see my wife, Emma, waving to me from under the tree in the shade; the stroller parked beside the blanket. It's perfect picnic weather, not a cloud in the blue sky. She has the sushi trays opened already, and we dig in.

Rollerbladers on the seawall whizz past, a young couple plays Frisbee, and a French bulldog chases a ball right past us. It feels like half of Vancouver is in the park today. And with weather like this, who can blame them? It's gorgeous. I lean across the sushi trays to check on my son, Samuel, still passed out in the stroller; his little chest is rising and falling.

Emma and I do the new parent chat about naps, schedules, and doctors' appointments. I mention the meeting with Vince.

"It's nothing," Emma responds, "he's probably just checking in to see how you're doing. It's not easy juggling work with a new baby." She smiles. "You are doing a great job. Hopefully, they will ease up on the overtime you've been doing."

"Yeah, that's it," I reply.

"Or . . ." Emma says, "maybe it's a raise!"

I'm back in the office with ten minutes to spare. I absentmindedly check my email inbox, read an old junk mail message, delete it, then check the clock: 12:56pm. I roll back from the desk, get up, and head to Vince's office. He'll notice I'm early.

I reach the door and knock twice. The door opens. "Hey, Brent," Vince says. "Follow me." He stands up and walks past me down the hall. Odd, we've always met in his office: informal, loose, casual. Vince is the most laid-back boss I've ever had, as friendly and approachable as is possible in this profession. During my job interview, we hardly even spoke about the position. Instead, we joked about all the different music we'd put onto cassette mixtapes back in the day.

But I wasn't getting that mixtape vibe today, that's for sure. He looked rough—unshaven; his shirt wrinkled and untucked. He walks ahead of me and makes no conversation. We pass through the foyer and past the reception desk, where the receptionist smiles. I nod my head at her as I walk, then follow Vince down a hallway. I've never been down this hallway before. Vince opens a door and holds it for me. I enter a room so small it only has three chairs set around a table. A blue folder is sitting on the table.

"Where should I sit?" I ask.

"Anywhere is fine," he answers and takes the seat on the right. I ease into the chair on the left.

"We need to wait for someone," he says, as if to no one in particular.

"Okay," I answer. I adjust my sitting position slowly, so it doesn't look like I'm squirming. The door opens, and a youngish guy in a brand new suit enters.

Vince waits until Suit Guy sits down, takes a second, and then says, "I'm sorry Brent . . ." He leans forward on the table, over the blue folder, still closed. "There's no other way to say this . . ."

I feel my gut churning.

"Today's your last day with the company," he says.

My mind spins. The ax had fallen. Everything moves in hyper-speed, but at the same time, it's like I'm watching myself in slow motion.

Vince continues. "I know this must be unexpected," he pauses. "I wish there was another way . . . but this has come from the head office. With the company takeover, the economy, and our budget cuts, things have been out of my control."

The three of us sit there, in the small windowless room, somewhere behind reception. I've worked in this building for three years, and until today, I had no idea this room even existed. Too small for a meeting room, I can only assume it's the company *dismissal room*. Many employees have probably sat exactly where I am now.

"So, today is really my last day?" I hear myself talking, my voice trembling. Vince said this already; I realize that, but I wasn't processing it.

"Yes, I'm afraid so," Vince answers slowly and deliberately. I could tell he hated this part, careful not to make a verbal misstep and violate company protocol.

"I won't be coming in tomorrow?" I ask.

"I'm afraid not," he replies.

I try again. "Is there another role I could transition into?"

"I'm afraid not," he shoots that down too.

"I know this is a lot to take in," Vince says, "you've always done great work here . . ." He pauses as if waiting for me to answer but carries on before I can say anything. "You can always reapply down the line if another job comes up."

I nod. "So, what happens now?" I mumble.

"We need you to sign a few documents, then we can discuss the severance package," he says. "And we can also connect you with a back-to-work program."

I start signing the forms like a zombie. Vince points out each section. "This one, and the one underneath, then the one under that." It's like a mortgage. Both Vince and Suit Guy were very thorough, making sure every section was covered in initials, dates, and signatures. By 1:34pm on July 17th, 2009, it was all over.

Suit Guy gets up, walks out the door, and tells me to follow him down the hall. We head down a staircase, a door opens, and suddenly I'm standing outside, in the back lane next to the loading bay beside the company dumpsters.

"What about my stuff?" I blurt out.

"We will schedule a time after-hours when you can collect your belongings," Suit Guy says. I'm dumbfounded. "Is there anything you need right away?" he says.

I squint against the brightness of early afternoon. "My sunglasses!" I exclaim. The sunshine, which had seemed glorious half an hour ago in the park, was now blinding me.

Suit Guy turns and heads back inside the door, closing it behind him.

What just happened? Shock, then confusion. What about Samuel? Mortgage payments, bills, diapers. I couldn't even fathom how I would break the news to Emma. It was the most important time in our lives. Now I was unemployed. How would we manage? We were in the middle of a recession, and I had no work experience in anything other than computer software, a job that had taken me nearly a year and five interviews to land.

Suit Guy returns, hands me the sunglasses, offers his condolences, and heads back inside. The door clicks.

I start walking, heading toward the Skytrain home. After a while, I find myself on a detour, sitting at a coffee shop, and start rehearsing how I would break it to Emma. It's not fair, I tell myself. I had nailed the art of working in an office: constantly over-performing and never once getting involved in petty office politics. I had even won an Employee Recognition Award last year.

I leave the coffee shop and head home, walking up the stairs, pausing in front of the door. I must have been standing there for a while because Emma eventually opened the door.

"I'm guessing no raise?" she asks.

"I'm out . . ." I start.

I go inside and sit down at the kitchen table. "Don't worry. Something will work out; it always does," she says. Emma is the Yin to my Yang, always the positive one. She still has ten months of teacher's maternity leave left. I hope I can land something before then . . .

I eventually make my way down to the garage with a beer. My Pioneer DJ mixer and decks are sitting in the corner on a table. This was my makeshift practice room and DJ studio, where I would spend hours daydreaming and mixing. *Glad I got these before I got the ax*, I think to myself as I turn it on and move a slider along.

The evening was a blur. It was midnight before I knew it. I crack a fourth beer, or was it a fifth?

My phone buzzes again. By mid-evening, I'd stopped checking it; too many emails and text messages offering condolences. Word had obviously spread. I try to resist, then break down and look at the screen. The subject headings all look the same.

Dude, WTF . . .

Are you okay?

I'm so sorry! I heard what happened!

Call me.

OMG, I can't believe it!

My head feels like it's on fire. I know if I go to bed now, I will have to wake up and face reality . . . and I'm not ready to do that yet. I check the clock; it's 1:12am. The feeling of being up this late on a work night feels decadent. One small luxury is that I don't have to get up early tomorrow. For the first time in a long time, the 6:00am alarm will not be going off.

I go upstairs to the fridge to grab another beer, and my phone buzzes again. I reluctantly check it. It's a message from Big Jay, the head of the social committee at a private tennis club on Vancouver's west side. Emma's been a member for a few years, and I'd done a few Friday night parties with my newly-purchased decks in exchange for free exposure and a free dinner.

I read the subject line: *Available to DJ a wedding in Sept?*

BLACKOUT

"I'm the DJ," I say to the doorman.

I've rehearsed these words dozens of times in the car on the way to the venue, but it's the first time I've said them out loud. It's my first paid wedding DJ gig, and I'm so nervous that I feel sick. Sweaty palms, rubbery legs, and feeling like I'm going to throw up is not the image of a cool DJ I had in my mind. The doorman at the boutique hotel, one of the city's swankiest venues in the city, looks me up and down. He's wearing a long wool coat and white gloves, cocking his head, then shoots me a look that says, *so what?*

"I'm here for the wedding," I say, feeling the need to explain myself. Instead of clarifying things, it sounds more like a question.

I swallow hard, then gesture over my shoulder toward my car, a Toyota RAV4, double-parked sandwiched between a Ferrari and a BMW. The doorman nods his chin. "You've got 15 minutes to unload," he says, "or it gets towed." He rolls a bellboy cart toward me. I grab it, smile awkwardly, then turn and push it toward my car.

I open the door and survey my sound gear—speakers, a mixer, plastic containers filled with cables—packed in and around Samuel's baby seat. As I lift the first speaker out and place it on the cart, it dislodges one of Samuel's stuffy toys from behind the car seat. It falls out of the car onto the wet pavement. I grab the toy and throw it back in, hopefully before anyone notices. I quickly pack everything else on the cart, shut the door, and roll it toward the entrance. The doorman pulls open the large glass door as I approach. "Liaison Room," he says as I pass. "End of the hall."

As I roll through the door, I instantly feel relief. Finally! Not being watched, now I can start . . .

BANG!

The cart collides with the other glass door, which I didn't realize was still closed. The entryway rattles, and I turn beet red with embarrassment. While people in the lobby turn and stare, and my heart is pounding, I straighten the cart and hustle down the hall. I arrive at the Liaison Room, quickly unload the gear at the dressed DJ table, and roll the cart back toward the entrance. The doorman is guiding a Mercedes into the valet spot. I return the cart and pass him my keys to park the car, then go inside to set up.

The groom is a friend of Big Jay who must have assumed I was also a wedding DJ, having seen me spin at the tennis club on Friday nights. He probably thought he was doing me a favor; the thought was there, but could I pull this off?

I'm about to lift a speaker onto its stand when I hear a commotion.

"The flowers are on the WRONG tables!" cries a female voice from behind me, and she sounds pissed off.

Ouch! I think to myself. *The staff sure are getting an earful. I would hate to be them.* I assume it's a wedding planner or banquet manager as I plug the speaker wire into the back of the mixer.

"These name cards are not organized properly!" She's practically shouting now, and the staff is scurrying around changing the place settings.

Wait, that doesn't sound like a wedding planner . . .

"Put the family photos at the entrance!" she continues, "not on the gift table!"

"Oh, shit," I say under my breath. I can now see the pissed-off yeller is wearing a white gown. It's the bride! Keeping my head down, I check the time: 4:18pm. There are still two hours until the reception starts. What's she doing here so early?

"You can't expect Uncle Dmitri to sit at the same table as his ex-wife!" she barks. "They must be moved—immediately!" She turns, then curses in an Eastern European language I don't understand. She's moving through the room, criticizing everything in sight. And she's headed my way!

My heart starts pounding. If she's raging over the place settings, what will happen when she finds out I'm an amateur? A fraud? My mind flashes back to the phone conversation when I told her I had done "at least 10 weddings" just to get the gig. What was I thinking?

She turns back toward the gift table and starts arguing about the floral arrangements. I seize the opportunity and rush out the door toward the bathroom before she can see me. I push open the door and run to the sink, feeling like I'm going to throw up. I splash my face with cold water, my legs trembling. What the hell am I doing here? This was a big mistake.

I stare at my reflection in the mirror, thoughts rushing through my mind, and I start getting angry with myself.

"You've never DJ'd a wedding before!" I say out loud.

Not only that, but I've only ever been to a single wedding before mine, in Cuba six years ago—and even then, I had no idea what was going on. It was in Spanish, for fuck's sake! Then I lean over, splash more water onto my face, and moan.

It's not too late to fess up. We can still call in a real DJ.

I hear a toilet flush behind me. The stall door opens, and an older gentleman walks over to wash his hands. I gulp another handful of water and wait for him to leave. He walks over to the hand towels and pulls the lever to dispense them. After what seems like an eternity, the door closes. I brace my hands on the counter and raise my head up again. I look at my face in the mirror, water still dripping off my nose.

"Okay Brent," I say quietly. "You can do this. Fake it 'till you make it." I grab a handful of paper towels, dry my face, and open the bathroom door.

I count 73 grumpy people. *Maybe it's the Eastern European influence*, I think to myself. When I visited that side of the world I noticed people seemed a bit dour, like the hardships of the past have sculpted their faces into a permanent scowl. I start the dinner music.

"Excuse me!" An elderly lady taps me on the shoulder, startling me. "Can you PLEASE turn DOWN the volume!" She says. "We are TRYING to eat!"

Flustered, I nod and make a grand gesture of pushing down the slider. She harumphs, then totters away.

Okay, maybe it's not cultural—maybe they are just grumpy old people.

I start feeling even more self-conscious. I cue up some soft jazz and err on the side of caution, keeping the volume at the halfway point. It sounds so quiet I wonder if I've gone too far in the other direction—I can almost hear them chewing their food—and I wonder if I'm losing my mind.

The meal seemed to last forever. Finally, after an agonizing 45 minutes, the servers appear and start clearing plates. There's a commotion at one end of the table, and a man in a suit stands up and starts walking toward me.

What's going on? My heart starts pounding. It's like that scene in *Jaws* where the shark is about to eat the swimmer, but she can't see it coming.

He's getting closer. What do I do? Suddenly, he pulls a folded piece of paper out of his pocket and heads to the podium. Of course—the speeches! I breathe a sigh of relief as he adjusts the microphone, clears his throat, and begins talking.

After what seems like an eternity, the speeches are over. The servers scurry around the cake table and prepare the large knife. Okay, at least this part isn't a surprise. I watch people milling around the cake, taking photos. The silence is awkward—should I play a song? I wasn't sure, so I just stood there.

"Ladies and gentlemen," the man at the podium says. "It's time for the first dance."

First dance? What? Am I supposed to have a song ready? Was I supposed to have checked with the bride before? My lack of wedding experience was showing, and I could feel sweat building on my palms.

I look over at the bride, who is busy organizing her dress. I madly flip through my collection, searching for a slow song. I'm drawing a blank when U2 pops into my mind. As the bride and groom approach the DJ table, I motion to them. "How about 'One' by U2?" I offer. "That's good for a first dance."

They nod indifferently and make their way to the center of the dance floor. Lucky break. I cue it up and press play. The first strains of the keyboard start, and the two dancers begin to move somewhat awkwardly. Bono's voice booms around the room.

It seems to last forever. Everyone looks bored. *Geez, I could've thought of a better first dance song,* I thought to myself, feeling my stomach beginning to tighten again. As soon as it finishes, I hear a slow clap at the back of the room. I did a quick headcount: 48 guests left.

"You can do this!" I said to myself. This should be the fun bit, playing cool music and showing off my DJ skills.

Collecting and playing cool music was always important to me. I wanted to be a DJ that was a connoisseur of discerning taste. Playing crowd-pleasers or songs you hear on the radio all the time is counter-intuitive to most DJs; we want to be creative and turn the audience onto new music.

I had spent the last few weeks downloading and organizing the latest club tracks in preparation for this wedding dance party. I was searching for hours for cool remixes and Top 40 mashups. I was finally feeling like a real DJ tonight, and so far, the mix was seamless. Here I was, the DJ, spinning on my brand new decks. I looked the part, and the mix was sounding awesome coming out of the speakers. There was only one problem. Nobody was dancing.

I tried to convince myself it wasn't me. *Maybe the crowd needs some time to get warmed up,* I thought.

As I'm flipping through my catalog for the next track, I see an older lady approaching me. She's in her 70s with a full head of white hair.

"Dear," she says, with a slight Irish accent, "could I make a request?"

"Sure," I smile.

"Would you please play some ABBA?"

There is no way I'm dropping ABBA right now. I've been hired to be the DJ, and right now, I'm dropping this UK deep house. The dance floor, on the other hand, wasn't appreciating it. I couldn't figure it out. It was number one on the UK deep house charts. I start to sweat. My job is to be playing music, to get people dancing.

So why the hell aren't people dancing? I think to myself. "Maybe it's just not a dancing crowd?" I say, trying to convince myself.

I need to find the right song for this crowd so they can get in the groove. Five minutes later, the older lady stomps toward me. This time she's not smiling. I get the feeling I'm about to be told off.

"Nobody's dancing!" she barks at me. The soft Irish accent has now disappeared.

"Y-y-yes, I know . . ." I stutter nervously, starting to explain.

"Play my fucking ABBA song now!" she interrupts.

My face burns up red.

"Sorry, I forgot," I apologize. "Coming right up."

I immediately load up the track while worrying about my cool quota.

The groom will kill me; any street credibility I may have had as a DJ is completely gone. My desperation could probably be heard bcoming out of the speakers as the piano intro swirl of "Dancing Queen" begins.

"Finally, some good music!" I could hear one of the guests shout. Within seconds the dance floor is completely full; most of the 48 guests are dancing!

The old lady was right. ABBA is *exactly* what this crowd needed.

How could she know this crowd better than me, I think to myself. *I'm the DJ!*

I shamefully push back the remix lined up on the decks to be played next, instead opting for Bob Segar's "Old Time Rock and Roll." The crowd loves it. They let out a collective, "Whoop!" and sing along during the intro.

And just like that, I discovered how to read a crowd. Quite literally, by looking out into the room and seeing if people were enjoying themselves. By studying the movements and subtleties of the dance floor I know what I love to play, but tonight I'm getting paid, so as long as people are dancing, that's fine by me . . .

The setlist had no order, no flow. I was shooting blindly, cringing at every track I played. But it seemed to work. I kept the crowd going with Shakira, Black Eyed Peas, Pitbull, and by dropping completely random requests to keep the floor packed.

Someone requested the Spiderman Theme song. "It's for my 5-year-old, he explained." Out of ideas, I shrugged my shoulders, quickly find it on YouTube, and play it.

Then out of nowhere.

BAM!!

Everything stops. The room is in complete blackness and totally silent. The music is off; the lights are out. "Did I overload the system?" I'm sweating. "I've ruined their wedding! I must have blown a fuse!"

The table-lit candles give me focus. I see the restaurant manager rushing toward the groom. He leans over and starts talking to him. The groom nods his head, then gets up and walks over to me. Thankfully he doesn't look too angry.

"A lightning storm," he starts, half laughing and shaking his head. "Total freak accident, the entire block is knocked out."

I breathe a long sigh of relief.

He writes my check by candlelight, confirming the spelling of my name. I look down at the numbers: $300 as promised. He shakes my hand. "You were great. Sorry we couldn't finish," he says apologetically. "Thanks for everything."

Divine intervention, I tell myself as I pack up.

I'm clearly not cut out for this line of work, but at least I've got money for the next little while.

CHAPTER 2

DON'T QUIT YOUR DAY JOB

A few weeks later, I was at the gas station, watching the numbers on the pump climb higher and higher. The recession of 2009 meant the job search wasn't going so well.

It sure would be great to book a few more gigs while I find another job, I think to myself.

Waking me from my daydream, I hear the thump of a car stereo system blasting tunes. A slick purple convertible pulls up to the pump next to me.

I watched the driver climb out of the seat: I recognize him from some of the club flyers around town. He's wearing a t-shirt branded with the GOODSPINZ logo.

GOODSPINZ, Vancouver's Best DJs!

If you're a DJ in Vancouver, you know this crew. They spin at all the big weddings, events, and celebrity parties in the city. You couldn't miss them. He must have known I was watching him because he looked up and gave me a confident smile.

Suddenly it all made sense. *If I can get on the GOODSPINZ roster, I'll be assigned to as many gigs as I want!* As my gas tank filled, I imagined how it would go down. I'd call the number and convince them to hire me. Soon, I'd be driving a car like that.

The handle clicked on my pump: $47.36. I wince, thinking about our dwindling bank account. I make a promise to myself to call GOODSPINZ when I get home.

I rush up the stairs and tumble through the door into the living room. I need to ace this call.

Ring. Ring. The line connects. An upbeat voice answers.

"Hello, welcome to GOODSPINZ!"

Momentary paralysis.

"Hello, can I help you?" the voice continues.

"Hi, my name is Brent," I blurt out. I steady myself, then continue. "I just saw one of your guys, and I wanted to give you a call . . ."

"Yeah, great," the voice continues, "saw one of the team in action, we get that a lot, you getting married? Need the best DJs in town?" The voice laughs.

In response, I laugh. This guy sounds like a used car salesman. I promise myself that I will never sound like this on the phone.

"So," the voice pipes up. "When's the big day?"

I take a deep breath. "Actually, I'm a DJ myself," I say, "I wanted to know if you're looking to add to your team . . ."

The line went quiet.

"Sweet, a true music lover!" The voice exclaims. "Where do you spin and how many gigs do you have under your belt, Brad?" the voice continues.

I cough. "My name is Brent, actually, but my DJ name is . . ." I start in.

"Listen," he carries on, talking over me. "I'm Hansen. Great to talk with you. You've shown initiative, getting in touch, so let's meet up."

Hansen is still talking; something about arranging a meeting tomorrow. But I'm already in dreamland fantasizing about the paychecks rolling in. I have to force myself to concentrate on wrapping up the phone call.

"Perfect!" I conclude. "Your office at 1:00pm. Thanks, Hansen," I add, using his name again—sounds more professional. "Looking forward to it!"

I'm at the front door of the downtown office a few minutes early, 12:47pm, a Grande dark roast coffee in my hand and butterflies in my stomach. I stare at the GOODSPINZ logo on the glass door for a few minutes rehearsing my spiel.

"Don't blow this, be cool" I tell myself.

At precisely 1:00pm, I buzz the intercom. Hansen answers with a confident swagger in his voice and invites me up.

As I enter the GOODSPINZ office he offers a firm handshake and a million-dollar smile. He looked like an old-school movie star, classically handsome with charisma by the bucketload. You know when he walked in the room, heads would turn. No wonder his company is off the charts with bookings; this guy has it. He's already my go-to wedding DJ, and he's barely spoken a word.

As we sit down at the meeting room table he launches in.

"I started 10 years ago when it was all word-of-mouth," he laughs. I laugh too, even though that's precisely how I've got all of my gigs to date. "Now it's all online booking forms and Facebook referrals," he says and tries on a different smile.

"Weddings, for sure, but that's just the tip of the GOODSPINZ iceberg," he says. "From suit-and-tie corporate events to film wrap parties and celebrity events," he says, in a voice that makes it sound like a tagline. "If an A-list movie star is getting married in Vancouver it passes through this office first. Every weekend, I've got guys all over the city spinning," he says, "giving the people what they want . . . right?"

He pivots the conversation. He asks about me, about my equipment and what kind of weddings I had done.

"Tell you what," he says after a few minutes, "We have a wedding this Saturday at the private members club around the corner. Come tag along, see the crew in action. Get a feel for the GOODSPINZ vibe."

I shake his hand, a smile spreading across my face. "I'll be there," I promise.

I leave feeling giddy. I aced it! Things were changing for the better. I could feel it.

Hansen was at the front entrance of the venue when I arrived—another overly-firm handshake. He led me across the freshly-waxed floor across the lobby into the men's bathroom.

The bathroom was bigger than the entire bottom floor of my house: heavy white porcelain sinks, polished brass, marble countertops, complimentary mouthwash, and hand lotion on the sink. There are no paper towels to dry your hands. Instead, there are soft cotton handkerchiefs. A shoe polishing machine sat in the corner.

He polished his shoes over and over again, making sure there wasn't the slightest trace of dirt and then told me how the night was to go. I was to shadow him and the team and see how things are done. Maybe I would get the opportunity to jump on the decks, show them what I got. My heart pounded. This seemed like a far more intense version of a job interview.

We walked back into the room; the party had started. One of his guys, a local high-profile DJ, decked out in a suit and tie, was starting the night off. I gave a nod and felt totally out of my element. The crowd looked wealthy, mostly older in dark suits and ballroom gowns. Hansen took me over the setup and talked about the flow of the night, including what lights he used, how powerful the speakers were, and how top of the line his equipment was. GOODSPINZ logos emblazoned on everything.

"Time to get this party rocking!'" he said, winking at me.

The DJ passed his headphones to Hansen as he jumped behind the decks. The volume increased. A Europop thump boomed from the bass bins with a flamenco guitar over the top. Hansen grabbed the wireless microphone and took his stance behind the DJ setup.

Putting on a deep radio voice, he shouted, "Ladies and gentlemen, are you ready to party?"

People on the dance floor, mostly an older crowd, agreed that they were indeed *ready to party*.

♫ *Hey, hey baby! Uhh, ahh! I wanna know, will you be my girl?*

Gulp. What is this song?

"Okay, everybody, put your hands in the air and repeat after me!"

He had dropped "Hey Baby," an Austrian remix of the 60s song by Bruce Channel featured in Dirty Dancing. Interesting choice, a little bit cheesy. I would never have thought to pull this one up. DJ Ötzi shouted from the speakers; Hansen continued waving his arms in the air toward the crowd.

He then mixed out of "Hey Baby" straight into "Cotton Eye Joe."

♫ *Where did you come from, where did you go?*

♫ *Where did you come from, Cotton-Eye Joe?*

Okay, okay, it's all good. This one is a bit overplayed, but it's all good, I thought to myself.

Hansen turned and motioned to me to get on the decks. I felt like I was back in elementary school with the entire class looking at me.

"What would you play right now, that the crowd is amped?" he shouted over the music.

I had no idea.

"Umm . . . something funky?" I shouted back. "Maybe some Aretha, 'Respect?' Stevie Wonder? Motown?"

"No way!" he said matter-of-factly. "We need some Y.M.C.A.!"

Y.M.C.A.? Hell no! That is one of the cheesiest wedding songs of all time. I learned at my last wedding that you need to read the crowd, but really?

I could handle one, possibly two of these songs in a row, but this was just too much cheese. The crowd was eating it up. He jumps over me and loads up the track, elbowing me out of the way. The song kicks in, the thin disco brass section and bass guitar boom through the sound system.

♫ *Young man, there's no need to feel down, I said, young man, pick yourself off the ground*

The chorus kicks in, "Everybody put your hands in the air!" Hansen shouts into the microphone.

♫ *It's fun to stay at the Y . . . M . . . C . . . A . . .*

He reaches across me to turn the volume all the way down so the crowd can sing along to the shout-out part. With every syllable, I die a little bit inside. It was too much. My face is burning up red. I suddenly feel aware and uncomfortable standing behind the DJ booth, the sweat dripping down my back.

"DO PEOPLE ACTUALLY LIKE THIS SHIT?" I ask myself. It was the sludge you heard in department stores and commercials. I wasn't sure if anyone was actually having fun or if they were just dancing because they felt obliged to. If this is what a wedding DJ was, then this was definitely not for me. My flight response kicks in, and I had to get out of there fast.

"Thanks so much for having me tag along; I really appreciate it," I told Hansen.

"Keep in touch," he yelled over the music. "I may have some gigs for you!" I wasn't sure if he was humoring me. Did he really want to keep in touch? It was obvious I wasn't a good fit. I didn't know what I was doing. If he does get in touch, I will have to be straight with him.

A remix of Kool and the Gang's "Celebration" echoes from the ballroom and down the hallway as I leave. I feel emotionally drained—head hanging low. I had wanted it to work but could I handle playing the Y.M.C.A. at every wedding? Maybe this wedding DJ thing was not for me. It was time for a Plan B. Now I just had to figure out what Plan B was.

When I got home, I cracked open a beer, told Emma about my night, and went straight to the computer to update my newly created website. Under the *Weddings* category, I created a Do Not Play List at the bottom of the page.

Do Not Play List:

- No "Y.M.C.A."
- No "Lady in Red"
- No Kool And The Gang, "Celebration"
- No "Cotton Eye Joe"
- No "Chicken Dance"
- No Santana, "Smooth"

I rocked back in the chair and surveyed my manifesto. Who knew? Maybe it would stick or even help me stand out amongst the DJ crowd. Not that anybody would actually see my website buried among the other hundreds of DJ websites when you did a local Google search of "Vancouver DJs." My site didn't even have flashy graphics or different pages to click, but I had to put it out there. It was cathartic.

But maybe playing the obvious cookie-cutter wedding songs I heard tonight was the norm? If I was going to DJ weddings, I had to put my foot down and remember this was only a way to make money.

A week later, the phone rang. Lauren and Joel told me that they liked my Do Not Play List.

"So, how many weddings have you done?" Joel asked over the phone.

"Ten!" I answered, almost too quickly.

They were impressed. I had all of my bases covered. I sent them a contract to sign that I had printed off the internet, adding to my professionalism. My price was based on other DJs in the city, and I planted myself right at the upper-lower end. Quoting $800, we agreed on $700.

A goofy smile covered my face, my first non-friend-of-a-friend wedding. I couldn't believe I was getting away with this.

That evening, the phone rang again. It was Hansen.

"Hey, how's it going?" he asked. "Listen," Hansen said. "I'm a bit short on guys next weekend. Any chance you are available? I can pay you $300."

"Thanks for thinking of me," I said, "but I'm actually already booked for a wedding."

"Really? Where?" his voice, a mixture of surprise and skepticism.

"Kirkland Barn," I replied.

"Lauren and Joel?" he asked.

"Yes, exactly!" I replied. "How did you know?" I was confused. There was a second of awkward silence on the other end of the phone.

"Lucky guess." Then a dial tone.

Lauren and Joel loved country music.

All that I knew was that another couple hundred bucks would keep me afloat for a while. I kept looking for another job, but during a recession, it might take some time . . .

Country music was not my forte, but I could cover the basics. I spent some time familiarizing myself with the typical country music wedding songs: "Save A Horse (Ride A Cowboy)," "Friends in Low Places," "Dust on the Bottle," "Fishing in the Dark," "Goodbye Earl," "Chattahoochee," and so on.

Dinner is done, and there are 200 people sitting in Kirkland Barn. It's the August heatwave, and the room is sweating, including me, and I have the added pressure of making sure I provide a dance party to be remembered.

I'm up on a stage overlooking the room, hopefully, nobody can see how nervous I am. I feel like I have to pee, or do I need to throw up?

Not only is it a hot day inside the room, but I'm sweating buckets, my shirt saturated with sweat.

Lauren and Joel stand in front of the crowd, ready for their first dance. I wasn't going to make the same mistake I did at my first wedding. This time I confirmed the name of their first dance song.

The MC announces the first dance, the crowd lets out their finest country "whoops" and "yahoos" and applaud as I start up the song. There is one problem: The couple isn't dancing. They are standing still with their arms wrapped around each other, staring at me.

I stare back at them.

Joel shakes his head back and forth. He mouths the words, "Wrong song!" at me while motioning the hand across his neck, cueing me to kill it.

I shake my head back and forth, "What's going on?" I ask myself, filled with confusion. I quickly fade down the song, jump off the stage toward them, with all 200 eyes on me as I approach the couple, still standing motionless on the dance floor. I really need to pee.

Joel's eyes are now bulging out of his head.

"Sorry, I don't understand," I start.

"Not the right song!" Joel loudly whispers. If looks could kill, I would be dead on the floor.

"But I double-checked, you wanted 'It Was You' from Trace Adkins, right?"

"Yes, but it's NOT what you played!" he responds.

"I'm so sorry," apologizing doesn't seem to help the look on Joel's face. Give me a second. I jump back on stage, looking at my laptop playlist: wedding song, first dance, all lined up perfectly. Wait . . .

The Trace Adkins song paused on my laptop is called "I Wish It Was You," not "It Was You." What the . . . how did this happen? *You had one fucking job!* I am screaming at myself silently while the entire 200-person room of guests stares blankly at me. That low-voiced cowboy motherfucker has a song called "I Wish It Was You" and another song called "It Was You." I scream in my head, *Who does that? Thanks a real-fucking-lot Trace Adkins!* Country music is often accused of being derivative, but this is too much to bear.

The room is dead silent. You could hear a pin drop. I'm not even sure what to do. I'll have to quickly find and download the correct song as quickly as I can. It will take at least a few minutes. My body is frozen, my face feeling like a rabbit caught in the headlights. I look over to the MC. Maybe he could help bide my time while I figure out what to do. He stands up, walks over, and grabs my wireless mic attempting to cover up the confusion.

"Ummm . . . sorry folks," he says. "There appears to be some technical difficulties." Shaking his head and rolling his eyes, he hands back the mic while leaning in.

"Hey pal," he says, whispering in my ear. "Don't quit your day job".

CHAPTER 3

MICHELLE'S WEDDING

My phone buzzes. It's a message from Michelle, a friend from XIZ. She'd worked there for nearly a decade—practically a veteran in the software industry.

"She's probably only now finding out I was sacked," I say to myself as I open the message. But it wasn't a condolence text. She was getting married, the text explained. They had been thinking of just playing music off someone's iPod, but then she'd heard through the grapevine that I was doing weddings . . . and so she was wondering if I was available.

I stop reading and start typing a reply, my fingers shaking.

Yes, I'm available and would love to DJ your wedding.

"This is it!" I say out loud. My ticket back into the company. This wedding was sure to be a "who's who" of the software industry. I'd be schmoozing, reminding the upper management I'm available for work, and also getting paid. "I could even bring some updated resumes and leave them on the DJ booth," I laugh to myself. Now, I had one job: to make sure this party rocked.

I head downstairs to the basement and stare at my DJ decks, left untouched for a couple of weeks.

"I can do this!" I tell myself; a surge of confidence washes over me. I switch on the equipment, crack my knuckles, and pull on my headphones.

I bypass the usual club tracks and cue up Stevie Wonder's "Signed, Sealed, Delivered." The opening guitar twangs bounce into my headphones, and Stevie sings:

♫ *Ooo baby, here I am, signed, sealed, delivered. I'm yours*

A wedding classic! My shoulders bounce to the beat as I'm getting into the zone, cueing up some more Motown. Marvin, Diana, and Jackson 5 boom from the speakers when I realize that the BPMs all clock in at 120, perfect for dancing.

How did I not know this before? I'm feeling so loose as I dance around to the tracks as if a higher power is making me choose the songs. Everything is coming so naturally. I jump to 70s disco, it feels good, and the mix sounds tight.

As I journey through the decades, I enter into the 80s. Next, I'm flipping through the one-hit wonders and guaranteed crowd-pleasers. As "Tainted Love" by Soft Cell builds to a climax, I hit stop on the left deck as he sings, "Don't touch me please—I cannot stand the way you tease . . ." adding in an echo effect on the mixer and bringing in "Don't You Want Me" by Human League on a dime, while snapping across the fader.

I catch a glimpse of the time. "Wow, it's 1:00am!" I pull off my headphones, rubbing my eyes. "I've been at this for four hours, time for bed." I shut down the equipment, head upstairs, and crawl into bed. "I'm ready for this!" I smile to myself, a feeling of confidence like never before as I drift off.

Guests casually arrive into the room and wander over to the open bar in the corner. Nobody's stressing over name cards on the tables tonight. This was a good sign.

There are girls in short skirts and high heels and guys with cool haircuts and nice suits. I recognize a few ex-colleagues and some managers. It didn't seem like anyone notices me, but why would they? The last time they saw me, I ran spreadsheets for the Sales Department—now I'm DJ BFAD.

Oh yeah, my new DJ name? That was all thanks to Britney Spears.

In 2004, she was briefly married to her backup dancer. It was all over the news. America's Sweetheart marries bad boy Kevin Federline, or as the tabloids called him, "K-Fed," using the first letter of his first name and last three letters of his last name.

While working at the software company, an A-type sales rep needed help closing a big quarter-end deal. It was nothing major, just correcting some paperwork and ensuring all the legal documents were in place. Because of that deal, he ended up exceeding his annual quota and making a mad commission.

"Yo, Beeeee-Fad is in the house!" he shouted down the office floor when it was all wrapped up. Soon I became the go-to person to help sales reps close their deals, and the name BFAD spread throughout the entire sales team. When word spread around the office that I was DJing on the side, I inevitably became DJ BFAD. All these years later, the name stuck. Who knew?

With my new DJ name and added confidence, I was determined to make it a night to remember for all the right reasons.

"You got this!" I tell myself, the positive self-talk psyching me up while loading the first track up onto the decks. During Cocktail Hour and Dinner Music, things just seemed to click. My set felt comfortable, no second-guessing, no hesitation. The volume was just right, and the song selections came naturally.

Then it was time for dancing. My mind goes blank. For a moment, I have no idea what to play.

Then I remember Stevie Wonder's "Signed, Sealed, Delivered."

Perfect, I think to myself as the opening chords ring out across the room. The crowd immediately fills the floor in front of me, justifying my selection. First, the girls drag their boyfriends and husbands, then the older uncles and aunts and parents. Within a minute, everyone is dancing! I follow up with some more Motown and 60s soul: Jackson 5's "I Want You Back," Aretha Franklin's "Respect," and Marvin Gaye and Tammi Terrell's "Ain't No Mountain." Nobody is leaving; the floor is packed. Soon I start plucking songs from Michelle's killer playlist she had given to me before the wedding and add them into the mix: Katy Perry, Lady Gaga, Rancid, Beastie Boys, Miley Cyrus, The Specials, Sublime, Johnny Cash, CCR, Bob Marley, The Cure.

I get on the mic congratulating the bride and groom, and let the crowd know I'm taking requests. A bridesmaid approaches, asking if I could play her song. "Sure thing," I yell over to her. "What do you want to hear?"

She yells back over, "Do you have T.I. 'Whatever You Like?' We all love that song; it's the bride's favorite!"

I'm not waiting around for the right time; I can already see Michelle dancing on the corner of the floor. I immediately load it up and drop the next song. The girls scream. The guys shout. It's an instant hit, and I'm stoked. I keep it going following it up with Hip Hop and Top 40. One song after another; I could do no wrong. The crowd is moving in unison to every beat, every drop. I have them in the palm in my hand.

A hand reaches across the decks for a handshake. It's Chris, one of my ex-colleagues! I return the handshake, a smile spreading across my face.

"Great to see you," he says. "What are you doing now?"

"This!" I laugh, pointing at my decks. *By Monday morning, my phone will be ringing off the hook with job offers,* I tell myself.

I was in the zone. All the stress of being unemployed, worries about money, sleepless nights surfing the internet searching for jobs all evaporated. It's an hour into the dance party, and the crowd is insane. Every song is getting more and more cheers of approval.

It's a lot of power being in charge of the music. Every touch of the volume, every single note of every single track is all on my shoulders. I can take the energy up to a hundred or bring it down to a nice and mellow chill vibe. If I played the wrong set or a bunch of songs for this crowd, people would leave. They would go home early, and the night would be over. But tonight, I'm reading the crowd right and playing the right songs for the right moments.

I drop the next song, and the crowd lets out a collective cheer.

"Oooooooohhhh!" That's how I know I've nailed it.

When the crowd has had enough and can't take anymore, I can see the energy dip; that's when I drop the BPM down and throw on more of a chill song. Something everyone can sing along to or give them time to grab a drink from the bar or hit the bathroom. The crowd needs time to recharge their batteries before I amp it up again.

The last half hour is pure adrenaline. My heart is pounding, my chest is heaving, and I'm sweating from every pore of my body. I feel like I can do no wrong when I'm in the zone. The crowd is loving it, arms around each other, loved up, and singing along to every song until the house lights come on at 1:00am.

When the last note of the last song is played, the crowd gives a simple chant.

"BEEE-FAD! BEEE-FAD! BEEE-FAD!"

I can't wipe the smile from my face and take a faux royal bow. A slew of handshakes, high fives, and hugs come my way before people reluctantly file toward the exit. Michelle comes over, grabs me by the shoulders, and gives me a giant hug.

"You killed it, buddy!" she says excitedly and hands me an envelope filled with crisp 100 dollar bills. "I'll definitely refer you!" she adds as she turns and heads toward the door. I pack up my gear, excited and high on adrenaline. I was hooked.

Could I really play music for a living and get paid? A few weddings a month, and I'll be raking in what I was at my last full-time job, be my own boss, have flexible hours, and most of all, get to play music for a living. What could be better than that?

Maybe being a full-time Wedding DJ wouldn't be so bad after all, I thought to myself on the drive home.

KILLED IT

Two weeks later, I get an email in my DJ Inbox. Jordan had seen me at Michelle's wedding and wanted to chat, leaving his phone number and a message to call him.

Who is Jordan? I wonder. *Does he work at XIZ? Is he hiring?* I quickly dial the number with curiosity and a newfound confidence.

"I saw you at Michelle's wedding. You were great!" starts the voice on the other end.

"Wow, thank you . . ." I'm still not used to compliments, but it sure is nice to hear.

"If you are available and up for it, I would love to have you DJ my wedding. It's a bit last minute, but it's in two weeks."

"I'm available!" I'm awestruck and can hardly believe it, another gig.

"That's great! After seeing you at Michelle's, I knew you were the right guy," he continues, "and honestly, you would be doing me a huge favor. It was on my Groom To Do List. I only had to book the DJ and get the groomsmen's tuxes. I've done neither so far. Typical groom hey?" he asks rhetorically.

I like this guy. I laugh, not knowing what a "typical groom" is; I've only had a few to deal with.

"I'd be happy to help you out," I reply. The truth is, he's helping me out way more than I can help him.

"Fantastic! It's at the Vancouver Convention Centre. They will already have a sound system set up. You just need to bring your decks and plug in. We have a singer/guitarist during dinner in another room, so at 9:00pm, we will open up the big room for dancing. Simple gig. 9:00pm until 1:00am, and if $1,000 is okay, you're hired . . ."

Holy fuck! I have to cover my mouth to stop it from blurting out. A thousand dollars and no equipment needed? This just keeps getting better. Without hesitation, I answer quickly before he changes his mind. This is the biggest no-brainer of my life.

"Totally, it all sounds great!" I say almost too keenly.

He pauses for a quick second before wrapping up the call. "Oh yeah, I almost forgot to mention, it will be a bit bigger than Michelle's wedding."

"No problem, how many people are you expecting?"

"Between 450 to 500 people . . ."

GULP

The blood rushes to my head. That's more people than all the weddings I've done so far combined. I had no idea weddings could have that many people. I must have drifted off and left him hanging. Jordan's voice brings me back to life.

"Is that okay?" he asks.

That money was way too good to turn down.

"Sure thing Jordan, I'll be there."

I've often heard, if you want to improve in a skill, you need to get out of your comfort zone and do something that scares you, right? Well, I guess I was about to improve, because I was petrified . . .

When I showed up for soundcheck a few hours before my set time, I somehow underestimated what a massive event this was.

The room looked like an aircraft hangar. My DJ booth setup was front and center of the entire room on a stage, complete with a 20-foot video wall behind me. Hundreds of floor and ceiling lights filled the room with custom-built decorations, specialty furniture, a lounge area, and five different bars. There were three sound and light technicians working with me and even a security guard making sure nobody came up on the stage.

Off to the side, there was a private Green Room with a couch and fridge filled with water, soft drinks, and beer. "DJ BFAD" was printed on the door. I felt like a celebrity. And I was instantly feeling out of my element.

Plugging into the massive sound system, the volume blew me away. It sounded so crisp and loud, much more than I was used to. There were a few minor technical difficulties as I patched my equipment into the system, which frazzled me even more.

After the soundcheck, I had two hours to kill before the party crew arrived in the room. The ceremony, reception, and dinner were in a different location in the venue. Nerves were setting in, and I was getting fidgety. Everyone, all 500 people, was coming to party with me; the pressure was on. I knew I needed to deliver the goods tonight. But was

I good enough? I went for a walk to Starbucks to chill out and grab a coffee, but my mind was racing.

What songs will I play? What will the crowd be like? What if I mess up? What if I bomb? What if they hate me?

On and on it went. I felt like I was going to throw up. I wasn't enjoying the calm before the storm. My head was spinning, and my heart was racing; I just wanted it to be over already.

I looked at my phone: 90 minutes before guests arrived as I walked back.

I was parked in the Convention Centre underground parking lot, so I decided to sit inside the car for a minute to catch my breath. I took a sip of coffee and flipped through some old CDs I had lying around in the glove compartment. There was an anthology of Elvis at the bottom of the pile. Hundreds of his songs burned onto a disc: the early rockabilly songs, cheesy Vegas stuff, his gospel albums, his movie songs. *He's a fellow Capricorn,* I thought to myself.

Did Elvis ever get nervous? Was he always that cool?

In a daydream, I took out a black Sharpie from my glove box and started scribbling on the back of the CD paper:

You killed it!!

I visualized the end of the night with people coming up to me and saying those exact words after the gig, just like Michelle did after her wedding. I was in a daze. When I snapped out of it, 15 minutes had gone by. My heart rate had slowed down, and I felt a calmness. The universe was going to help me tonight, I knew it.

I quickly drank my coffee and went back into the venue, a bit more relaxed and ready to go. I lined up some songs I thought would be good party starters and waited . . .

The start time had come and gone.

9:01pm

9:11pm

9:18pm

9:26pm

The wait was torture. Finally, I hear a commotion outside and the doors open . . . 9:32pm and the first few people come into the room. Maybe 50 people, it's time to start the show.

They are coming in hot and immediately hit the dance floor. I plunge straight into some upbeat dance music; there's no time to waste. A few start making early requests and grabbing drinks; everyone is laughing and already having fun. *This is a great sign,* I think to myself. Half an hour later, there are 200 people, and the room is starting to swell.

Two of the bridesmaids approach the request list. "Can you play Wilson Phillips' 'Hold On?'" they ask enthusiastically.

The 90s pop singalong by Wilson Phillips next; they insist. Bridesmaids are always top of the wedding request list pecking order, and I can probably work it into the current song I'm playing.

"Sure thing, next song!" I tell them.

As soon as I drop it, the crowd immediately goes off. They know this one. Hands in the air, arms around each other, a full-on power ballad singalong, and it's only 10:20pm. I was hoping this would be an epic night, but this was blowing the doors off any of my expectations.

The same two bridesmaids return 20 minutes later, drenched in sweat and mile-wide smiles. "Thanks for playing our song!" they both say. The shorter of the two leans in closer.

"Let us know if there is anything we can do to make your night better!" she yells over the loud music.

"Sure thing," I reply, tilting my head to the side in case I misheard.

"You know, anything to enhance your night?" the taller one laughs. "It starts with an M and ends in a Y."

Money? Wow, my first tip!

They look at each other, laughing. The bass from the speaker is booming right beside my ear, and I can barely hear them. The shorter one leans in, cupping her hands around her mouth.

"MOLLY!" she shouts.

"Ecstasy?" I laugh it off and politely decline. No wonder everyone is going off tonight. I just thought my set was super tight.

Regardless of which drugs or alcohol are consumed tonight, I feel in control.

By 11:00pm, the place was PACKED with over 500 people. There were people everywhere I looked. At the bar, in the back, at the side of the stage, in front of me, and everyone was wall-to-wall dancing and partying. The place was going insane. By midnight, I knew this was one of the best nights I had ever had.

To the side of the stage, I see Jordan. He gives me a huge smile and the double thumbs up. He whispers something to the woman with a clipboard under her arm standing next to him. Minutes later, she is standing beside me.

"I'm Misha, the wedding planner," she introduces herself with a confident smile. There was a look of curiosity on her face as she tries to find out which DJ company I worked for.

"I've not seen you on the wedding scene before," she says.

"I'm kinda new at this . . ." I admit.

"Well, New Guy, this is one of the most epic parties I've ever seen!" she replies. She immediately wanted to hire me for a wedding she had a few months down the line. "Oh, and by the way, it's Jordan's sister's birthday at midnight," she tells me, "maybe you could make an announcement."

I decide to do one better. I fade down the song playing and jump on the mic. Public speaking is not one of my strong points, but the adrenaline pumping through my body made me do the unthinkable. I gathered the crowd and organized an impromptu 500-person chorus of "HAPPY BIRTHDAY" for Jordan's sister. The singing in the room was deafening. Afterward, the crowd erupted in applause, and I knew just the perfect song to play to keep the party going.

♫ *Go, go, go, go, go, go*

♫ *Go, shorty*

♫ *It's your birthday*

When the night was finished, a wave of euphoria washed over me. I stood in disbelief that the night had unfolded the way it did. It felt like only 10 minutes had gone by. A bartender collects half-empty drinks from the side of the stage, "Hey buddy, awesome job!" he shouts to me. I give a nod, but it doesn't seem real. Am I dreaming?

One of the sound techs jumps up onto the stage, and I thank him for his help. "You made my job easy," he replies. "You have no idea how many shitty DJs I've had to sit through," he says as he wraps up a cable from the booth.

When I finally got back into the car, it was well past 2:00am. I noticed the note I had written on the back of the Elvis CD only a few hours earlier.

You killed it!!

It was a self-fulfilling prophecy. If only I had known, I wouldn't have been so nervous. Sweaty, tired, and with a huge grin on my face, I had formally made my decision: I was now a wedding DJ.

BROTHER WANTS TO DJ

As the weeks and months progressed and 2009–2010 recession plowed on, I never got a call for a job interview at my old company. It didn't matter though, Jordan's wedding absolutely cemented my decision to become a fully-fledged wedding DJ.

How could I go back to a nine-to-five job while working weekends? This meant more time watching Samuel and being a stay-at-home dad while being able to party all weekend. It was a win-win situation. Now I just needed more gigs. I racked up the credit card debt, bought some mobile DJ speakers and Revo club lights on stands, and I was good to go.

The thing about being a Wedding DJ is that nothing ever goes as smoothly as you think it will.

"The bride's brother wants to DJ for a bit during the party," Misha, the wedding planner, informs me.

It's two weeks before the wedding. Misha and I are doing a pre-wedding reception check-in, going over the itinerary, making sure we are on the same page and that all the music boxes are ticked. It's the usual stuff: guest arrival time, last call for the bar, the number of guests.

And now I'm thrown a curveball with the fact that the bride's brother wants to DJ. This definitely isn't a normal request.

Thoughts race through my head as I try to calm myself down. Who is he? Is he a professional DJ? Will he be bringing his own equipment or using mine? Will his skills blow me out of the water? What if the crowd loves him and hates me? It takes time to build up the crowd. What if I do all the legwork, and then brother takes over to get the glory?

"So . . . he's a DJ?" I ask nervously.

"No, no, no, he's the bride's brother," Misha says as if repeating herself will make me feel better.

"I mean, is he a DJ on the side?" I clarify.

"I don't think so," she says, explaining that he bought some brand new equipment and wants to play a set in the middle of the party.

It's not an ideal situation, but if the bride wants her brother to play, she's the one paying the bill, then who am I to dispute it?

The room is warming up for dancing as the 300 guests finish dinner and grab a drink from the bar and start hitting the floor. The room is massive, with the raised stage and hundred-square-foot dance floor at the end of the room.

The brother is in his early 30s; his clean-cut looks and sharp suit remind me of an investment banker and not the DJ image that I was expecting. He approaches me to the side of the stage. He's wearing a large black backpack with a cardboard box under his arm. I can immediately see the writing on the side of the box. It's the latest version of Pioneer DJ Controller, the professional ones used in clubs. He probably spent over $3,000 on it—worth more than mine. I start to sweat.

"How's the crowd tonight?" he asks like a true pro.

"Oh . . . uh, good . . ." I reply, caught a little bit off guard, not sure how to respond. "I'm just getting started, really."

"Great, getting them warmed up for me, thanks, pal!" he says as he steps beside me, putting down the box and taking off his backpack. He sets up his equipment to the side, brand new fresh out of the box—probably three times more expensive than mine.

"Top of the line," he winks at me as he pulls out his brand new Mac laptop from his backpack.

I immediately feel inadequate.

"Fade out your song. I'm ready," he nudges me out of the way.

I slide down the volume of my track as he lines up his first one. He shakes his shoulders, cracks his knuckles, and gets into DJ mode. A small crowd of friends and family gather around in front of the dance floor.

"Wooooooooooooooooooo!"

They yell in anticipation. The brother holds up his hands, fingers, and thumbs connected to make a heart shape. His audience is ready to party as he starts his set. Electro-indie-beats fill the room.

"Whooooop! Yeeeeeeeeeaaaaahhhh!"

I start getting nervous . . . *what if he kills it?* I think to myself. What if everyone loves his set, and they don't want me to come back on?

He's the brother. He will know his audience better than me! My mind is racing. *I will look like a fool. They paid me to be here and . . .* I stop myself and decide to grab a beer to calm my nervous energy.

Luckily nobody at the bar recognizes me as the DJ. I'm sweating as I order a beer, the bar area is packed, and it takes a few minutes to get served. I don't want to be known as the DJ that got shown up by the amateur relative on the decks.

The conversation in the room sounds louder than before I got to the bar. I turn around to face the dance floor and see it evaporating. The hundred spectators just five minutes and two songs ago are now at around 20 people.

Little by little, the dance floor is evaporating.

The beat matching is on-point, and the BPMs haven't changed an inch. The song selection is smooth, but this crowd is NOT feeling it. Within 20 minutes, the dance floor is completely empty—not even one person. Three hundred people are at the bar and chatting around the room at peak party time.

One of the guests eventually recognizes me as the DJ and grabs my arm. "Hey, when are you back on?" he asks.

"Another hour, I think . . ." I answer, not actually sure myself. "Whenever the brother is done."

"Ugggghhhhh," he moans to his friend; they roll their eyes.

"What do you want to hear when I get back on?" I ask.

"Biggie, Tupac, Kendrick, any Hip Hop, not this SHIT!" he yells toward the dance floor. His friend laughs, and they clink their beer glasses. I take a mental note of his requests and walk back toward the side of the dance floor.

One of the other guests nods toward me.

"Hey, you were good, mate," she says with a British accent, her husband beside her smiling.

"Oh, thanks! Anything you want to hear when I get back on?"

"Jamiroquai would be nice. New Order, The Killers?" she tells me. Another request list mental note.

I go back to the DJ booth pretending like I forgot something in my DJ bag. The brother is sweating bullets. His look of earlier confidence is gone. His eyes are bugging out of his head—a deer-caught-in-the-headlights look on his face. I know that look well; I've had it for every gig for almost a year. What do I do next? How do I get them back? Thoughts race through your mind. No rational decisions can be made. Do you change tempo or change genres completely? It's trial and error until you hit the sweet spot.

He grabs my shoulder. "Hey, maybe you could take over a bit earlier," he asks.

"Are you sure?" I say, "I don't want to interrupt your set."

"I've practiced this for weeks," he confesses, staring at the empty dance floor. "I thought I had it down." His bedroom setlist was on-point mix-wise, but he was not reading the crowd, as I had learned the hard way.

I'm secretly happy that he is bombing.

"Okay, I don't mind jumping on a bit early."

Now I need to try to resurrect this dead floor, I think to myself. And I know just what to play! I look out into the crowd; the Biggie guy and his buddies are looking at me. One of them gives me the finger-to-eye motion, indicating, 'I'm watching you, don't mess up!'

Brother fades down the tropical house beats.

I give it a few seconds. The tension builds as I select and line up my track. I know that this will give the crowd what they want, but then I have a moment of self-doubt. What if the party is over and the dance floor is completely unfixable? I will look like a fraud, no better than the brother.

There's a moment of hesitation, and then finally, I hit play. The opening bars of Notorious B.I.G.'s "Hypnotize" fill the room. I push it louder than I should, tweaking the higher reaches of the yellow, almost tipping into the red, for added effect. The crowd lets out a literal roar as they run toward the floor.

"Man, you sure know what you're doing," Brother says while folding up his laptop and hastily throwing his equipment back into the box.

"Thanks for warming the crowd up for me," I say.

"Nothing to do with me," he confesses. "You're a pro!"

Only a few months ago, I was told not to quit my day job. Suddenly this DJ thing, this wedding life, was my *new* day job.

So far, so good . . . what could go wrong?

THE PARTY

CHAPTER 4

A DAY IN THE LIFE OF A WEDDING DJ

12:00PM	SHOWER, GET READY
12:30PM	LOAD UP CAR
1:00PM	EAT LUNCH, GRAB COFFEE, LAST-MINUTE CHECKS
1:30PM	LEAVE
2:00PM	ARRIVE AT VENUE
2–2:30PM	UNLOAD, MOVE GEAR & EQUIPMENT FROM CAR INTO ROOM
2:30PM	MOVE CAR FROM LOADING ZONE TO LONG-TERM PARKING
2:45PM–4PM	SET UP, GET READY, SOUNDCHECK
4–4:15PM	LAST-MINUTE TOUCHES, SOUNDCHECK COMPLETE
4:15PM	DOORS, FORMAL GUEST ARRIVAL TIME

5:00PM	CEREMONY START TIME
5:30PM	CEREMONY OVER, COCKTAIL RECEPTION STARTS
6:30PM	MC ANNOUNCES, GUESTS FIND THEIR SEATS
6:45PM	MC WELCOMES GUESTS, VENUE HOUSEKEEPING RULES
7:00PM	MC ANNOUNCES COUPLE, GRAND ENTRANCE
7:05PM	WELCOME SPEECHES
7:10PM	DINNER OR BUFFET SERVED
8:30PM	DINNER FINISHED, COFFEE SERVED
8:45PM	CAKE CUTTING
9:00PM	GRAB DRINKS, FRESHEN UP
9:15-9:30PM	COUPLE'S FIRST DANCE
9:35PM	PARENT'S DANCE
9:40PM–12:45AM	DANCE PARTY
12:45AM	LAST CALL
1:00AM	LIGHTS ON, PACK UP
2:00AM	HOME, UNPACK CAR
3:00AM	GRAB LATE NIGHT SNACK, BED

Once I made the decision that I was going to be a wedding DJ, things happened fast.

Together with Emma's income, we could gauge how many weddings I needed to pay the mortgage and buy some food. Being a stay-at-home dad during the week and a wedding DJ on the weekend meant we also saved money on childcare. The severance pay from XIZ had long run out, but I was able to make as much as I was at XIZ for less than half the work.

As my reputation grew, so did the bookings. It gets challenging to keep track of all the couples, ceremonies, receptions, and locations. Still, in every case, I made sure I gave my blood, sweat, and tears for each and every couple, whether it was 50 people at a community hall or 300 people in the city's most prestigious hotel. Every wedding would be a night to remember.

I started to get couples booking me a year in advance of the wedding day to ensure they had me and that their party would rock. Mother-of-the-brides would come up to me at the end of the night, grab my face, and kiss me; they were so happy. I started spinning for entire generations of families getting married, the brother would hire me and then the sisters. I was getting to know them and started to feel like a member of the family.

Some weekends, I could pull in three weddings—one on a Friday, one on a Saturday, and one on a Sunday. It was all about supply and demand. Once I was busy and known to be a killer wedding DJ, I was able to up my prices, now pulling in between $1,000 to $1,500 a night.

It was perfect. There was no overhead and no expenses aside from the equipment, speakers, and lights I had recently invested in. The hours were long, but the pay was right. No more worrying about picking up that extra piece of cake for dessert. No more worrying about filling up the tank with gas.

As with any job, there were massive learning curves. I mean, when a stranger full-on belches in your face, you deal with it. Some of it wasn't ideal, but if it meant I could pay the mortgage and not go back to working in an office, then it was good for me. My wedding days average 12 hours from start to finish. I'm the first one at the venue and the last one to leave. I see guests arriving all fresh and polite and crawling out on all fours at the end of the night when they are too hammered to walk. They're long days for sure, but they're always worth it when you get the fat paycheck at the end of the night.

Complete strangers have trusted me, DJ BFAD, with the soundtrack to the most important day of their life. And I will do my best to make sure it's everything they have dreamed of.

Well, that's the plan anyway . . .

THE FULL BEER INCIDENT

I watch as he approaches the DJ booth.

Eyes glazed over, slim build, and wearing a suit that doesn't quite fit, a size too big like something borrowed from his brother's closet. In his left hand, he is carrying a plate of half-eaten wedding cake. As he gets closer, I notice he looks exactly like the comedian, Tom Green, and also that the entire front row of his teeth is missing.

"How long are you playing old-people shit for?" he shouts over the DJ decks, smelling of freshly smoked BC Bud.

"I get it; this music isn't your jam," I tell him, promising to change it up soon.

"Dude, my song next!" he says, though I can barely hear over the speaker beside my ear.

The night has just begun. We have plenty of time for his request, a country line-dancing song.

"Yeah, soon!" I shout at him over the booming bass from the speaker beside me.

He mumbles something about it being his favorite wedding song. I nod my head, trying to hurry up and end the conversation so I can cue up the next track.

"Sorry, I can't hear you!" I shout back, leaning forward, placing my hands over the decks as my eyes dart down to the track, counting backward, about to end.

(00:01:07)

Every second counts, and this guy is completely oblivious. He keeps talking. I lean closer, hoping for some way to end this conversation so I can cue up my next track.

Suddenly, a large piece of half-chewed chocolate cake flies out of his mouth. It lands on my hand with a splat and sticks there. He doesn't notice and keeps rambling.

I stare down at the lump of his chewed-up food on my hand. My brain is doing backflips, and my hand is frozen and twitching. The dime-sized chunk sits there on the arch between my thumb and index finger.

I scream at him in my mind. *Swallow that fucking cake before you talk!* I say professionally with a smile, "I'll try to get to that one later!"

As he walks away, I recoil my hand, looking down at the digital display.

(00:00:37)

There are no tissues or napkins around the DJ booth to wipe my hand. I get the idea that I can shake it off, flapping my hand violently while trying not to send the blob flying toward my face—no small feat. Unsurprisingly, I'm unsuccessful. It's stuck like glue.

I panic-glance around, looking for something to remove it, spotting my request list on the table in front of me. I wince at the thought, then rip a page off, smearing the cake and sticky saliva off my hand. I ball up the paper and toss it aside, still feeling the sticky residue in the spot.

(00:00:03)

Muscle memory takes over. I watch my right hand dart out, snap on the cue button, spin the jog wheel 45 degrees, then hit play. That same hand shoots onto the mixer, flicks the effects switch to phaser, then tweaks the shit out of the dying second of the song as the funky bass line of the next song surges out of the speakers.

I run to the bathroom to grab a handful of paper towels. When I get back, I decide to throw on Trashed Guy's line dancing song.

"Let's get this over with," I tell myself. I don't want him coming over here again.

You often hear about people who have had traumatic incidents who can recall time slowing down, and every detail is super vivid. It's caused by the part of the brain called the amygdala that controls memory, decision-making, and emotional reactions. If you have ever experienced this, you will often think, if you were to relive that exact moment over again, what would you have done differently?

As soon as the first notes of his request blast through the speakers, I see him perk up and attempt to run toward me. During the excitement of hearing his song he gets off on the wrong foot and trips mid-step on the dance floor.

The full pint of beer in his left hand launches from the glass.

It looks like a scene from the movie *Rambo*. Sylvester Stallone runs toward the camera while a hand grenade explodes behind him, and he jumps toward the camera in slow motion. I can see the beer flying toward me, but I'm helpless as it completely empties over me, my shirt, my table, and worst of all—my DJ gear. He is momentarily stunned sober while I stand there in disbelief, dripping wet. That's when I notice;

it's eerily quiet in the room.

The power light on the mixer is blinking, the CDJ is completely soaked, and there's an error message on the digital screen.

I frantically try to grab some of the restaurant staff for some rags and cloths, anything to wipe it all down. Bridesmaids in their matching pink outfits, with hands on their hips, demand to know what I'm doing, stopping their line dancing song halfway through.

"Why are you stopping?" one bridesmaid screams.

"Sorry, everyone, technical difficulties!" I shout out to the room; my voice cracks with nerves.

Okay, this isn't as bad as it looks, I tell myself. Maybe if I turn everything off and on again, it will be fine. As I attempt to turn everything back on, a spark flies out of the back of the mixer. It's completely drenched.

Trashed Guy is now apologizing and trying to help mop up the mess, stressing me out even more. My head is going topsy turvy; what do I do?

"Keep it going, bro!" someone else shouts.

The bride is now standing inches from my face. "What time are you supposed to finish?" she demands.

"I'm sorry I can't go on," I say, pointing to the damaged equipment and then to the culprit standing beside me.

"Lucas! What did you do?" she screams toward him.

At this point, I'm uncertain what I'm going to do; the blood rushes to my head. This is unprecedented territory. In retrospect, I know I should have a full set of emergency backup equipment, but right now, I don't.

The "boos" echo throughout the room become deafening.

It feels as if time is standing still, but I decide the only thing I can do is get out of there. I desperately throw my stuff together. Wires, cables, power cords, and decks that are usually all packed with care are now rammed into the bins dripping wet.

I'm sweating profusely, losing confidence fast. A crowd of guests gathers around me, wanting an explanation.

"Where are you going?"

People are getting understandably angry. I'm trying to keep my cool while explaining the situation and offering an apology. There is nothing else I can do.

If I had any backup equipment, I could take a five-minute break to collect my thoughts and re-plug in, but I don't. In the meantime, the quicker I can gather my things and get out of there, the better.

The only way out of the venue was inconveniently located via the heavy double doors right beside the bar. Since the dancing had stopped, the next logical place for the crowd to go was to grab another drink. The entire reception had congregated at the exact location I needed to be leaving from. This meant squeezing and pushing up against the very people whose night I just ruined.

I couldn't fit all my equipment in one trolley load, which meant I had to make three separate trips. It was the longest 20 minutes of my life. By the time I get the last trolley full of equipment out the door, the guests' hurling insults were getting louder; it was almost deafening.

"Worst DJ ever!"

"Amateur!"

"You fucked up the party, bro!"

But hey, what doesn't kill you, right? Always bring backup equipment. No matter how short or potentially low-key the gig is, bring a second set of decks, a spare mixer, headphones—everything. Going forward, I also added a legal footnote to the contract.

"Brent Faddies shall not be held liable for any action or losses arising from or in connection with the provision of the DJ Services under this agreement by any persons not directly affiliated with Brent Faddies. Furthermore, the Client agrees to assume full responsibility for any and all damages caused by the Client, his or her agents and/or guests, to any of the property of Brent Faddies."

This wasn't the last time something like this would happen. But this time, I would be prepared.

CHAPTER 5

SINKING SHIP

The Starbucks barista smiles at me as I approach the counter. "What can I get for you today?"

"Large dark roast, please," I reply.

I've stopped at this Starbucks a few times a month for the past year. It's a short drive from my house. I've got the routine down on my way to a wedding. I can pull in, grab a coffee quickly, and be on my way fully fueled up.

She punches the order into the cash register. I open my wallet. "On my card," I say.

"So . . . enjoying the sunshine today?" she asks, watching me insert my card into the machine.

"Unfortunately, I'm off to work," I say while entering my PIN.

"I can relate; I've been stuck in here all day," she continues. "What do you do?"

"I'm a DJ," I reply tentatively, knowing what's about to come next.

"Wow! How cool!" she instantly perks up. "That must be such an awesome job!" I feel my face turning red as she continues. "Tiesto is my absolute favorite! I was just at Shambhala last weekend!" She squeals, unable to hide her excitement. "Which clubs do you spin at?"

She's in for a big let-down in 3 . . . 2 . . . 1 . . .

"Well, actually . . ." I say, "I'm a wedding DJ," The space between my collar and neck gets hot. I watch her face change, unable to hide her disappointment.

"Oh . . . neat . . ." she mumbles, thrown off-track by my revelation.

"Yeah," I say, "it has its moments." I grab my coffee and head off to my wedding gig.

4:30pm

It's half an hour until the wedding ceremony. I tape down the last speaker wire as the guests start to arrive inside the venue in suits and ties.

I notice a commotion over by the coat check. It's nothing too peculiar, simply a guest trying to take off their jacket to hang up in the coat check.

After a few seconds, it catches my eye. He's struggling to take his coat off. Tugging at an arm, he pulls it with such force it throws him off balance, and the arm comes off inside out.

He then takes a few misplaced steps and stands at the bar, negotiating to get a shot. The bartender is still setting up his station and smiles at him, saying the bar is not open until after the ceremony.

Damn, he's starting early, I think to myself and chuckle.

It was still half an hour until the wedding ceremony started, but he was already drunk. *Must have hit the bar next door,* I think to myself and laugh. I nickname him Drunk Guy and make a mental note to keep an eye on him throughout the evening. I take a deep breath and load up some pre-ceremony music—soft classical on low volume as the guests mingle.

Drunk Guy is not mingling. He heads straight back to the bar and stands at the counter, craning his neck, looking for a server. At least he'll sober up a little during the wedding.

I scan the crowd but find my thoughts returning to Drunk Guy. Is he a guest? A plus one? Perhaps he's a distant cousin or a friend from University days invited out of politeness?

This is how I usually spend the first part of an evening: people watching. I try to imagine their life stories and how they are connected to the couple. Relative, co-worker, high-school friend, neighbor? When I get stumped, I just make something up that's entertaining; it helps the evening go by faster.

8:03pm

Dinner has been served, and the waiters are clearing the finished plates. The bottles of wine on the tables are long gone, and people move toward the just-opened bar. Drunk Guy is the first in line, leaning far over the counter and speaking to the bartender.

Once he has a drink in hand, he turns on his heels and strides toward me.

As he approaches, he starts talking, oblivious that I can't hear him over the music. He puts down his drinks, extends a hand, and slurs, "Hey brother . . ."

I try to avoid shaking hands with drunk people. It's a death trap; once they've got a physical hold of you, they rarely let go, rambling in your ear. I try to ward him off with a fist bump instead, but he doesn't comprehend, and our hands misconnect. It's awkward.

"How's it going?" I ask.

"Fucking good man!" he says.

"Anything you want to hear?" I reply, cutting to the chase—no need to beat around the bush.

"You got some of that old school west coast SHIZZZZZZZ?"

"Sure do!" I say. I know exactly what he wants. Mid-90s California Hip Hop, but it's a bit too early.

"It's only 8 o'clock. Let's wait a little bit," I suggest.

He looks annoyed. "I'm ready now, bro!" he says, louder. "Drop that shit!" he replies.

"I know," I say as if confiding in him. "But I don't want to throw down anything too heavy before the first dance," I say.

It takes a bit of time to sink in, and then he says, "Okay, I'll be back in 15 minutes."

It's going to be a long night.

As he leaves, I cue up another track. I'm moving the tempo slightly more upbeat, from laid-back chill to more funky stuff. I watch the crowd, searching for signs that it's loosening them up. Shoulders shake, heads bob, and feet tap.

Ten minutes later, the bride and groom approach the floor for their first dance. I get ready, my finger hovering over the volume slider. I cue up their song: John Legend's "All of Me." I must have played this over two dozen times as the first dance the last couple of years. Every wedding season, there is one song that takes the "First Dance Most Played Song Award" this year goes to John Legend. Previous winners have included Jack Johnson's "Better Together," Jason Mraz's "I'm Yours," and Ed Sheeran's "Thinking Out Loud."

Once finished, I cue up some funky jams to get the party started and play some Motown Stevie Wonder, Aretha Franklin, and James Brown. As the horns blast and James Brown kicks it, I feel a physical change of energy in the room. When I look up, with my headphones still on and the music blasting, chaos is erupting right in front of me.

Then the smell hits me.

That unforgiving sour, acidic aroma of vomit. It's so strong my throat starts to tighten up, and my eyes start to water. The room quickly turns into a holy mess. People are running in different directions, and the dance floor is cleared while my mind tries to process what is happening.

One of the bridesmaids is covered in vomit, with chunks of partially digested food dripping down her arm. I see Drunk Guy standing next to her, covering his mouth with his hand, puke running down his sleeve.

The crowd recoils in horror. A group of girls rush to the vomit-strewn bridesmaid and circle her like an entourage covering a celebrity from the paparazzi. They quickly escort her to the bathroom.

"Ommmmmigod!" I hear one of them yell as they run past.

Drunk Guy is off in the distance, wiping his mouth with his sleeve. He makes a coughing motion and covers his mouth as a small amount of chunky pink liquid oozes through his fingers.

I have a strong stomach, but the smell is almost unbearable.

My eyes water, nostrils burn, and throat contracts. I feel like I'm going to be sick myself, but I can't leave. I try to plug my nose with one hand while keeping my other hand on the mixer.

Sadly, this isn't the first time someone has puked on my dance floor.

My Top 3 Wedding Pukes

1. The bridesmaid who stumbled through the front doors and projectile vomited into a garbage can before the reception even started.
2. The uncle, who slammed back too many drinks during dinner, smashed his head onto the dinner table while people were still eating, cradled his face, and spewed inside his arms.
3. The teenager who ran across the dance floor with tightly-clenched hands covering his mouth and a look of horror in his eyes as he desperately tried to make it to the bathroom. No longer able to hold it in, he opened his hands and sprayed chunks all over the dance floor.

This is, however, the first time someone has puked on another guest, which, by all accounts, seems a bit more dramatic.

I check my phone; it's 10:08pm. There are three more hours to go before I can pack up. I start to take a deep breath and instantly gag, the smell hanging heavy. I sigh, keeping the beats rolling while the room is in chaos. What else can I do?

I'm the equivalent of the band on the Titanic, still playing music while the ship slowly sinks.

Half of the guests get their jackets on to leave, Drunk Guy is being escorted out of the room, and everyone else is scattered anywhere but near the dance floor.

One thing I've learned over the years is to never assume a scenario like this is going to unhinge or end the night; it usually doesn't. The DJ just has to roll with it. I've been paid to be here. From the start to the bitter end, although some nights end earlier than others . . .

SHOTS!

My left index finger twitches on the volume control while my right is ready to tap *start*. I'm about to drop "Shots" by Lil Jon and LMFAO. It's an obnoxious rant custom made for college dorm parties and people who want to have a soundtrack while they drink shots.

The song just doesn't seem to fit my surroundings.

I'm at one of the most exclusive high-end venues in the city. The massive room is absolutely decadent: 7,000 square feet with 23-foot high ceilings, crystal chandeliers, and gold leaf on the plaster-cast wall moldings.

I tried to work out how much was spent on this wedding which included:

- three videographers
- three wedding planners
- two photographers
- 300 guests
- 6,000 dollars' worth of flowers (at least)
- a gigantic video wall with the couple's image towering over the room
- an AV tech

- a four-course five-star meal
- an open bar
- a five-tiered wedding cake
- a photo booth
- live musicians during cocktail hour

My best guess? It would pay for a nice chunk of a down payment for a multimillion-dollar house in Vancouver or a least a luxurious trip around the world.

I've played this intro what feels like a million times.

Lil Jon screams.

♫ *If you're not drunk ladies and gentlemen! Get ready to get fucked up!*

I cringe. I forgot to download the edited version of the song.

Hopefully, nobody noticed, I think to myself.

I have the song cranked as much as possible as I try to conjure up some energy into the room, the lights on the mixer almost hitting the red.

♫ *Shots! Shots! Shots! Shots! Shots! Shots! Shots! Shots! Shots! Shots! Shots! Shots! Shots! Shots! Shots! Shots! Everybody!*

♫ *The ladies love us; when we pour shots; they need an excuse; to suck our cocks!*

Damn, I wish I remembered how bad these lyrics were.

The grandparents sitting at the table in front of me shake their heads, looking at me like I'm an idiot. A kid at the next table over giggles while his mom tries to cover his ears. My face is beet red with embarrassment.

A request from one of the groomsmen, I thought it would be a great way to kick off the party, but it's not like in the movies where you drop a song and people go crazy. You have to build it up slowly over the night and pick the right moments. Bad judgment on my part. This doesn't feel like the right place or time.

The bride signals me to pass her the mic.

"If you're not drunk ladies and gentlemen, get ready to get EFFED up!" she yells towards the roomful of guests. The bride and her immediate circle of friends hit the bar on the other side of the room. They order a round of shots and down them in one gulp.

The bride and groom are sweet, quiet people. During our consultation we went out for ice cream cones. That's why this seems so out of character. But they had wanted a big party for all of their friends. I briefly spoke to the bride during dinner. She looked tired.

One of the videographers told me she was up at 4:00am getting ready and putting the finishing touches on the day. She started getting her makeup done at 7:00am and the dress fitting shortly after that. There were lots of getting-ready photos, breakfast photos, and the first look with the groom photos. The ceremony was at 2:00pm, and now here we were at 9:05pm.

About an hour into the party, the banquet manager, rushes toward me.

"You can announce the last call now," she blurts out as she approaches my table.

“What?” I say in disbelief. I check the time on my phone. “It’s only 10:27pm!” I tell her, showing the screen. The last call isn’t until 12:30am, over two hours from now.

“We’ve had a small change of plans,” a look of concern on her face.

I take off my headphones and quickly scan the room; I see the blur of a white dress from the corner of my eye.

It’s the bride.

Her arms around her bridesmaids as they prop her up and carry her out of the room. The entourage wobbles down the hallway in their flip flops, the groomsmen following behind holding their girlfriends’ purses and shoes, while the groom is at the back with an armful of wedding presents.

So much for those shots! The long day, stress, and lack of food have taken their toll on the exhausted bride.

As I announce the last call for drinks, I lower the volume and thank everyone for coming out.

“Congrats once again to the bride and groom!” I announce at 10:28pm. It feels surreal.

It doesn’t matter how much people plan or spend on their wedding day, when the bride is frog marched out of the party, it’s officially over. Hey, I’m happy I get to go home early and still get paid for a full night. But there is also a lack of satisfaction that I haven’t fully rocked the dance floor.

GRAND PIANO

The groom steps up to the piano. It's not just any piano—this is the grandest grand piano I have ever seen in my life: ivory white and freshly buffed, sitting in the middle of the dance floor.

The room is completely silent as he starts the tender, gentle ballad for his new bride. He gently sings an Adele song. The entire song lasts just under a minute.

I barely have enough time to take it in; then it's over. As the last note rings through the room, the guests erupt into applause.

He slowly stands up as his new bride runs into his arms.

The five hotel staff standing in the wings rush in to wheel the piano out of the room. Earlier in the day, the grand piano was delivered up two flights of stairs delivered by five guys, covered and wrapped. It takes four people to move it in. The hotel staff set it up and take off the covers.

One song only. That's it, and the piano is done. I'm trying to figure out how many thousands of dollars that minute cost.

The entire room is white, containing white flowers, a white dance floor, and white curtains. There are full bottles of Hennessy and magnums of champagne on every table. The bling is everywhere—on outfits and the opulent decor. There is a lot of money in this room.

I'm in the corner. I'm only scheduled to DJ for 30 minutes while guests arrive before dinner and an hour at the end of the night. There is a live band playing during dinner, but I still charged full price. Sometimes I have to justify my costs. This couple didn't even flinch when I quoted. The total amount was paid in cash in an envelope.

We initially met for the consultation a few months ago at a coffee shop on Main Street. There were a few emails back and forth about hiring me to be their DJ, but nothing was set in stone. As soon as we sit down, they slide over an envelope full of cash. There's no contract signed; nothing agreed upon. *This sure is trusting,* I thought to myself at the time.

Washing my hands in the bathroom before I was about to start, I notice tattooed necks, Armani suits, and Rolex watches. The guy washing his hands beside me has a freshly swollen black eye, his fingers covered in gold rings. These are some truly scary-looking guys. Larger bottles of Courvoisier, Macallan, Crown Royal, and Jameson are on each table, as well as a fully-stocked open bar.

I'm due to finish at 12:00am. It's a hard strike, meaning I can't go a minute over my finish time. The room will be taken down, and they need everyone out as quickly as possible. A hard strike is a DJ's favorite—no second-guessing or playing for an extra amount of time. Once it's midnight, it's all over.

"Thank you, everyone!" the MC signs off for the night. "Please take home the table vases." It's 11:41pm. The wedding planner standing across the room looks in my direction and twirls her finger. *Hit it, DJ.*

I have less than 20 minutes to play a mix. If I'm lucky, maybe I can cram in five or six songs before midnight. I opt to choose the first song from the bride's Must Play List, an EDM remix of a Coldplay song. The room is already in full tear-down mode. Nobody is going to dance tonight. The band is packing up their equipment while the decor vendors are coming to collect the pipe and drape displays around the room. I play another EDM remix from the Must Play List. Guests are grabbing their jackets from the coat rack beside me. The bride and groom are saying their goodbyes. Five songs in, and the wedding planner is back.

"Okay DJ, you're done."

The easiest money I've ever made.

Weeks later, a nice five-star review appears on my website. Some gigs are a piece of cake, some not so much.

SMOKE MACHINE

The groomsman was trying to be helpful; he really was.

He had a clear vision of how the dance floor action should go down. He wanted a rager. At what point should I have told him that it's probably not a good idea to have a smoke machine on the dance floor in an old building that doesn't have opening windows?

"Hey DJ, I brought a smoke machine," he tells me while setting it up in the corner.

"Do we need it?" I ask skeptically.

"For more ambiance, like a nightclub!" he says, like a kid with a new toy, hitting the big green button, which makes the smoke come hissing out in a thick blob.

"This room is tiny, and we can't even open the windows. Don't want the fire alarm going off. The lights should be fine." I offer.

He insists. We have a smoke machine, and we are using it. He showed me how to work it, telling me to hit the green button every ten minutes or so.

When the dancing starts, I hit it once. The dance floor collectively *oooohs* at the novelty of the sudden appearance of smoke.

"More smoke!" the groomsman shouts from the dance floor, signaling with a twirly finger.

I hit it again.

While concentrating on the big green button, I notice the beat of my next song didn't come in right on time; the crowd also notices. It was a sloppy mix. I decide to concentrate on the beats and put a hold on the smoke. Growing frustrated with the lack of smoke, Groomsman Bro eventually comes behind the DJ booth and starts hitting the green button that controlled the smoke machine himself.

The sweet-smelling fog begins making my eyes water, getting lodged in my throat. It was now so thick I could barely see my decks, using one had to cover my mouth coughing, while the other was on the cross-fader.

Three minutes after the last blast, the groomsman approaches again.

"We need more smoke!" he shouts in my ear over the music as the machine hisses into action again.

"Dude, I'm trying to spin music. I'm not bothered about the smoke machine; I can barely see," I shout back.

"It's better for the ambie . . ." he starts. Our conversation is interrupted.

BREEP-BREEP-BREEEEEEEEEEEEEEEEP

BREEP-BREEP-BREEEEEEEEEEEEEEEEP

BREEP-BREEP-BREEEEEEEEEEEEEEEEP

The look of enthusiasm on his face drains, replaced by a sheepish look—a look of somebody who just ruined his best friend's wedding dance party.

The on-site building manager rushes in.

"Everyone out! We need to evacuate the building; the fire department is on the way!"

The crowd quickly disperses as I sit in eerie silence at 9:42pm on a Saturday night. A beautiful empty room covered in balloons, flashing disco lights, and settling smoke as the sound of a fire engine approaches in the distance.

You can't say I didn't warn them, but then again, most clients don't listen to the DJ.

CHAPTER 6

HANNAH'S WEDDING

Hannah met me at 12:30pm sharp in a coffee shop at the base of an office tower downtown. She was on her lunch break, she explained and was very appreciative I could fit into her schedule.

"They say you are the best," she says as we sit down. I thank her, blushing slightly.

The conversation is smooth, effortless. We discuss my arrival time, the set-up location, and the event timeline. Then I ask her about music.

"Anything you want to play is good," she replies. "You are the professional, after all." She checks her phone and smiles. "I'm happy to book you," she says. "Send me your contract when you get a chance, and we can lock this in." We smile, shake hands, and she heads back to the office.

I open the cafe door with a spring in my step. Maybe it's the coffee buzz, but I'm feeling absolutely great about this gig. September wedding, some of my favorite vendors, and a low-maintenance bride, what could be better?

"Wouldn't it be nice if all brides were like her," I ask myself as I cross the street.

Two hours before the ceremony, I pull up to the venue in my Toyota RAV4, newly furbished with my DJ BFAD logo on the side. I'm feeling confident and ready to rock another epic party, especially with a bride as laid back as Hannah.

We had a few emails back and forth a couple of weeks before the wedding. She had sent me a very long Do Not Play List. I was a little surprised. During our meeting, she had been indifferent about the music. Oh well. "Must be those wedding day jitters," I tell myself.

As I'm loading in my DJ equipment through the venue's front door, Michael, the wedding photographer, rushes by in a hurry with his head down, almost knocking me over. I manage to catch his eye and give him a smile. "Hey Michael, everything good?" I ask.

We have worked over a dozen weddings together. You couldn't meet an easier-going laid-back dude, but not today. There is a look of frustration in his eyes as he shoots me a quick look as if to say, *nope, not all good.*

Moments later, Misha, the wedding planner, rushes out. Making direct eye contact with me, she swears under her breath as she passes by me.

"I'm going to fucking kill someone," she whispers.

"That bad?" I say. She stops, pivots, and leans in close to my ear.

"Seriously, had I known this shit was going to go down, I wouldn't have taken this job!" she says and continues to speed walk out the door.

Seconds later, the wedding entourage bursts into the room. Four bridesmaids in neon pink dresses are already hammered. Good thing they brought their own booze. They will be cut off at the bar soon enough. One pulls a flask from her handbag, opens the lid, takes a swig, then passes it behind her to Hannah, who is following behind. She grabs the flask, takes a giant swig, and hollers, "It's my wedding day, beeeeeyotches!" She looks more like one of the Real Housewives of Beverly Hills than the shy, slightly nervous soon-to-be bride from a few months ago.

"Hey, it's the DJ" she snaps her fingers toward me and keeps walking. The bridesmaids all cackle, giving each other high fives.

It's always the quiet ones.

Everyone has a different idea of what "The Best Day of Your Life" looks like. For some, it's about having a small intimate, low-key affair with your nearest and dearest. Others choose to go with all the bells and whistles.

Hannah's wedding had it all: decorated place settings, seating charts, symmetrical candles, bursting floral bouquets, wedding favor take-homes for the guests, and birdcage cardholders on the gift table. In addition to me, she'd hired a musical trio for the ceremony and an after-dinner pianist. The ceremony and reception were supposed to run from guest arrival at 5:00pm until the Grand Sparkler Exit at midnight. At a typical wedding, that's a great tight timeline, but tonight there were far too many moving parts crammed into the day. There are only so many hours to squeeze everything into; instead of having a day with lots of neat surprises, things could easily turn into a sloppy mess.

One of the caterers mentioned the bride had raised her voice to one of the waiting staff. I struggled to connect the quiet, shy bride-to-be with the larger-than-life diva passing by me. Maybe she got caught up in the hype? Maybe the pressure was too much for her? Maybe she was always a finger-snapping control freak, and this was her excuse to unleash it?

The loud A-type personalities hardly ever go Bridezilla. But something gets triggered in the quiet ones. A pent-up emotional state of being well-behaved for so long snaps, and they are given free rein to act like the Queen. Just like alcohol brings out your true self, so do weddings. It's like the quiet co-worker who you go out with for drinks who turns into a raging lunatic, downing Jägerbombs, swinging off barstools, and starting arguments with the lady from Accounting.

Hannah spent the entire day just looking for an excuse to complain. I mean about EVERYTHING.

She complained to the catering staff that guests were using the wrong plates for their hors d'oeuvres.

The wedding cake wasn't cut properly.

The cucumber water didn't have enough ice.

The room was too warm.

It went on and on.

"Seriously, is Hannah the most miserable bride ever?" I ask Misha.

"Why is it always the quiet ones?" she replies with a shake of her head.

The Maid Of Honor had approached me; her plan was to do her speech just after the Grand Entrance. "I'm so nervous, sorry I can't make my speech now. I hate public speaking. Can I wait? Can I do it later? I'm sorry, I'm just so nervous," she tells me.

I show her how to use the mic, which button to press to unmute it, and where to hold it while she's talking.

"Maybe I'll have a little drink first to calm my nerves," she says.

A few hours later, she snatches the mic away from the MC.

"Awwwwwwwwwwwright people, lemme tell you sumthin'!" she turns and points to Hannah. "I love this bride!" then raising her voice, "I motherfucking love you!" There's a gasp from Grandma in the front row. "Whoops, sorry for swearing," she snickers and then continues for another ten minutes telling drunken ad-lib stories that don't seem to have an ending. The MC attempts to take back the mic. I give him a nod and kill the volume.

"Don't take the mic, hold on, I just have one more thing to say. I love this fuckin' bride!" He manages to snatch the mic and hands it over to the Best Man. She finally flops back down in her chair while he nervously pulls a piece of paper from his jacket pocket.

"Ladies and gentlemen, ahem," he clears his throat. "I'm Drew, the best man." A few people applaud.

"I'm sure you'll agree that Hannah looks absolutely stunning today, while Eric, on the other hand, just looks stunned," There are a few giggles from the audience.

"They say the best man speech should only last as long as the groom lasts in bed (slight pause); goodnight, everyone!" A few hands clap.

"Okay, enough with the jokes. As you all know, the groom is handsome, witty, intelligent . . . sorry Eric, I can't make out the rest of your handwriting," The one-liners are coming thick and fast. He continues.

"I think every man in the room will agree with me when I say that today is a sad day for us all, knowing that a woman like Hannah is now off the market. I also think that every lady in the room will all also agree with me when I say that today has just passed without a ripple!"

Oh geez, come on, Drew! These jokes are all straight out of Googling *How to Write A Best Man Speech.* I've literally heard these a hundred times before.

He then launches into a few stories about how they grew up together, some "wild and crazy" nights they had in University, and how he has never seen Eric so happy before—finally ending with a guaranteed line that's been used in every best man speech.

"Hannah, place your hand on the table, Eric please place your hand on top. Enjoy this moment. It's the last time you will have the upper hand." Polite claps and fake laughs from the audience ensue.

A few more speeches are given, and I'm ready to pluck my eyes out. I would completely be ignoring these if I didn't have to ride the mic volume. They go from talking too quietly, causing dead air, to shouting into the mic and causing feedback.

When Hannah and Eric step up for their speech, I know it's almost over, thank goodness.

"Sorry we haven't written anything down; we're just going to wing it!" she tells the hundred plus guests.

Little did anyone know, we were about to witness the longest thank you speech I had ever witnessed—over 31 minutes, to be exact.

They were repeating stories and making up toasts on the fly. I'm fairly sure nobody was listening. I checked out after two minutes. I had a feeling this was going to be a long one, so I quickly took a bathroom break and grabbed another coffee. When I got back to the DJ booth, Hannah was in the middle of telling the same story.

You could see the crowd getting fidgety.

"Puuuuuuuuuulease, end this already!" I shift in my chair, stifling a yawn.

The vendors and staff roll their eyes at each other after each story. We have heard every single one of these told before at various weddings by different couples. According to the timeline, as soon as their speech was finished, we were going straight into their first dance. So, I waited. What else could I do?

Excruciating boredom.

"COME ON! We are literally dying from this speech!" I scream in my head. Death by boring wedding speech! Bring on the Zombie Apocalypse!

I drift off, daydreaming about the zombie movie I watched the night before.

I start ranking all my favorite zombie kills. Then, my favorite zombie-killing weapons. If I were in a zombie apocalypse, which weapon would I choose? Chainsaw or machete? Baseball Bat or samurai sword? Noooo, a baseball bat with spikes on it . . . what's that called?

I pull out my phone and do a Google search*:* *baseball bat with spikes*

Bingo!

Hundreds of pictures pop up. I see one I like on the second row. Instead of a baseball bat, it's a steel club with a ball on the end covered in spikes. "Yes, that's the one!" I say to myself, clicking on the image and reading the description underneath.

"The morning star club is a medieval weapon consisting of a spiked ball mounted on a shaft, resembling a mace."

Ahhh, the morning star; that sounds so badass.

I think I would have a machete strapped to my leg and a morning star on my back, maybe some ninja stars! Yeah totally, zombie movies never have ninja stars! I would carry around 20 in a pouch. Practicing every day for an hour or two, on a tree, until I was a ninja master. They would hit the target on the tree at lightning speed.

ZING! ZING! ZING!

The brain eaters would have no idea what hit them. Then I would run up and smash them in the head with my morning star.

SMASH!

Wait, there's some coming over the hill. Maybe fifteen or twenty . . . it's too late to run, but I'm ready. I unbutton the machete from my leg holster for extra killing power. The walking dead slowly get closer and closer, growling and hungry for flesh.

They surround me. It's GAME TIME. I grip the morning star tightly with both hands, and my knuckles tense up. They circle me; it's do or die, and I've never been more ready . . .

"Ladies and Gentlemen, it's time for the bride and groom's first dance!" A voice snaps me back to reality, and I cue up Extreme's "More Than Words."

The first dance is over 8:30pm, but instead of kicking up the dancing, we are given a performance—a piano singer named Sapphire.

Hannah spotted her playing at a hotel lobby bar last weekend and just had to have her here tonight. Another impulsive last-minute bride request. Sapphire was to play until around 10:00pm. She played a beautiful selection of downtempo romantic modern ballads with the voice of an angel. Unfortunately, the drunk dudes listening to the beautiful sounds of Adele and Norah Jones cover versions were not cutting it. The room was getting rowdy.

Soon, she had lulled them into such a blissful state, they didn't feel like dancing. Instead, they went out to smoke BC bud, leaving the room completely empty. As Sapphire packs up her portable keyboard at the end of her set, Hannah gives her a big hug. "Thank you so much! You were amazing!" she squeals.

I started playing to an empty room just after 10:00pm. There is absolutely nobody on the floor. Stifling a yawn, I start my set. I am due to finish at midnight. That gives me just over 90 minutes to turn this into a wild night to remember. But right now, the room is cold; there's no audience, no motivation, and no good music on the playlist. I will need to work some miracles.

Misha pops over to the DJ booth a few songs in, shaking her head in frustration.

“Just a reminder from Hannah,” she says, “there are to be absolutely no songs played for her parents or older guests.”

“Ugh, she’s not giving me a lot to go on here, and I need all the help I can get,” I tell Misha. But she already knows. She gives me a knowing smirk and tells me to work with what I have.

To make matters worse, Hannah wasn’t even in the room. She was outside on the patio, socializing and getting more photos with Michael, the photographer. Not to mention her Grandma is still sitting at her table and giving me the evil stares as I drop Top 40 song after Top 40 song to an empty dance floor.

As guests start leaving, I hear a commotion to my right at the staircase.

An older man, I think Hannah’s uncle, had fallen down the stairs. He couldn’t get up, was in a lot of pain, and needed the paramedics. Misha tells me he twisted his ankle.

“Great start to the dancing,” I sigh.

A bearded hipster struts up to the DJ table, my first request of the night.

It’s the bride’s brother. Skinny jeans rolled at the ankles and a tweed suit jacket—pure thrift store irony.

“Hey man,” he says. “Can you play ‘Pumpin’ Blood?’”

“Ummm . . .” I can’t even fake I know this one; the look on my face must have said it all.

“You know,” he continues, “by Nonono?”

"Riiiight," I say slowly, feigning comprehension. Nonono, I don't know that band or song.

"And it has to be the Belarbi Remix," he adds. I wince.

"Ah, *that* one," I say. "Sorry, I don't have Belarbi remix."

"Okay then," he concedes, "just play something by Odesza."

I raise my eyebrows.

He snorts. "Chairlift?"

"Can you write it there?" I say, gesturing my request list. I don't have any of his songs, but I need to appear like I'm making an effort. "I may be able to get to it later."

He scribbles a few lines, then heads back to the dance floor. I lean over to take a look: MÖWE, Attom, Junip, Bear Mountain. "Damn," I mutter, "I don't have . . ."

Suddenly he's back. "Oh," he says, "totally forgot. We need 'Holding On' by Flume. It's the bride's favorite!"

"Nice!" I say. Never heard of it. I take a swig of coffee. Looks like a long night ahead.

As soon as he steps away, the groom's Aunt Agnes approaches the DJ booth, reeking of stale cigarette smoke and vodka. She grabs the pen from the DJ Request List, and scribbles down a song.

She mumbles something about also playing "Old Time Rock and Roll" and stammers off into the crowd. When I lean over to pick up the Request List, the smell hits me!

I've been crop-dusted.

It's a serious industry hazard. Someone comes over to the DJ booth, drops a fart, and walks away. Meanwhile, the DJ is left there, unable to move while the lingering green smoke wafts around us. The smell remains while the crop-duster has long since departed.

Most wedding food consists of heavy carbs, roast beef, possibly some asparagus, and coffee, and the DJ can be a sitting duck. If a guest decides to let one slide out while writing down a request, I'm a goner. It can linger, sometimes for minutes. I'm obviously unable to escape, so I can only plug my nose and choke back.

Crop-dusting is a no joke and tonight was worse than usual.

The toxic smells seemed extra thick and beefy; the rich, thick steaks had made the guest's bowels gurgle. I always smell it more when steak dinners are on the menu. Fresh farts wafted through the restaurant and everywhere in the room. Nowhere was safe. It was in front of the bar, near the entrance, beside the Photo Booth, and especially in the bathroom. At least everywhere else, there was a chance of escaping, but standing here behind the DJ booth? I was a goner.

Michael's wedding photographer assistant is walking toward the DJ booth.

Keep walking, keep walking, I visualize.

Her bag of backup camera equipment is right beside the DJ booth, so of course, she heads right toward me and the rank aroma encompassing the entire six-foot radius.

As soon as she gets within a foot, the heavy, obnoxious odor of beefy fart hits her. Her expression instantly changes; her nose crinkled up, eyes squinting.

"Wow!" A nervous laugh escapes me. "Does that ever smell . . ." while wafting the air in front of my nose dramatically with my right hand.

She coughs and covers her mouth with one hand while grabbing the camera bag with the other.

"Damn . . . the groom's aunt," I try to shift the blame, but it sounds more like an admission of guilt. "She was here a second ago," I look around frantically. Aunt Agnes is long gone, so I can't even point her out.

She doesn't say a word, changes her camera lens at Mach speed, and ducks back into the crowd. I felt like yelling into the microphone, "Damn you and your stinky ass, Aunt Agnes! I didn't even eat the BEEF tonight!"

I continue to waft away the toxic gas for the duration of the next song when a short, dark-haired lady in her 60s approaches the DJ booth.

"I'm the mother-of-the-bride." I get the impression she does not care for my set so far tonight, nor does she look like the type of mom you would mess around with. "I would like to hear some Elvis," she says.

I quickly scan Hannah's Do Not Play List sitting on the table.

- No Hip Hop
- No House, EDM, or Club Music
- No Classic Rock
- No 60s
- No Elvis

"Strange, Elvis is actually on my Do Not Play List from the bride," I tell her. I should know better. A side-eye from mom insinuates I had better play it next.

"I'm the mother-of-the-bride," she states again, very bluntly in case I missed it the first time. "If it wasn't for me, I'm sure we wouldn't be here right now, and I would like to hear Elvis next."

Ouch, I swallow hard.

The worst thing about it is that she's right, and I'm stuck in the middle of some serious family politics right here. For a minute, I internally debate both sides. *Do I respect the person paying my bill tonight, or do the right thing and play the mother's request?*

"Jailhouse Rock" it is.

Hannah won't even notice; she's outside mingling with her posse, and hey, *maybe this will strengthen the mother-daughter bond,* I tell myself. Hannah's mother is immediately out rocking on the dance floor, strutting her groove thang. Score!

About a minute into the song, Hannah walks by on her way to the atrium with her entourage. She shoots me a look that confirms I have made the wrong decision. It says, "My wedding, my day!"

Sweat is gathering on my neck.

Do I continue with the Elvis 50s and 60s theme, or do I pull the plug? I decide to yank it after Elvis and put on one of Hannah's requests—The Killers, Kings of Leon, or some other 2000s indie band. The main problem is that now she is in the atrium outside and doesn't even hear it. The people on the dance floor, including Mother, are less than impressed and evacuate immediately.

The dance floor is struggling. I'm struggling. Requests are coming in, but it's everything on the Do Not Play List—Hip Hop, Electro House

Music, Classic Rock, 60s, and of course, more Elvis. My default excuse, "Sorry, it's on the bride's Do Not Play List," is starting to wear thin. These drunk-ass guests don't care about her Do Not Play List. Hell, they don't even care that much for Hannah, by the looks of it.

I'm frantically searching for the next song while the counter display on the left deck is quickly counting down until the end of the current track. I need to load up another song quickly and mix it in.

0:38 seconds

0:37 seconds

0:36 seconds

Decisions, decisions . . . Aunt Agnes' "Crocodile Rock" request or Uncle Larry's "Footloose" request? I flip a mental coin. Footloose it is! I've played this song at so many weddings I know it like the back of my hand. There's no need to cue it up; simply load it onto the left channel, hit play, and fade up.

0:18 seconds

0:17 seconds

0:16 seconds

Here we go! Volume up on the left channel, volume down on the right. Nothing fancy.

The crowd lets out a collective groan, and most of them leave. Damn. It bombed. The wedding cheese is too much on this one. Uncle Larry gives me a big thumbs up. This crowd is putting me through my paces tonight. There are 2:56 minutes left of this song before I try again to win them over.

As I scan through my tracks, I can feel a body beside me. It must be Aunt Agnes back again asking for her "Crocodile Rock" request. There is now a hand on my left butt cheek. I jump, startled, and snap my head to the side. It's one of the bridesmaids.

"Oh, hey!" I say, surprised.

"Hi," she says in a sultry voice.

"Um, anything you want to hear?" I offer while trying to maneuver my butt cheek from her kung-fu grip.

"Nope," she responds, her glassy-eyed gaze fixed uncomfortably on my eyes, completely oblivious. I'm trying to get her out of my personal space without being a jerk.

"Sorry, I'm going to have to just concentrate; let me know if there is anything you want to hear," I offer politely, trying to squirm out of her grasp.

Footloose is approaching the one-minute mark. Time to find the next track.

"Sure," she says, oblivious to the strong hints I'm dropping. I'm so annoyed that I can't concentrate.

"I'm just going to get the next track lined up," I tell her.

"Here, let me help you," she reaches over and starts touching the laptop, her right arm around my waist. I can't take it anymore.

"Seriously, I can't spin! I need you to get out of here!" I tell her.

"So, I'm annoying you?" she snaps.

"Sorry, I don't mean to be rude, it's just that I'm trying to . . ."

"ASSHOLE!"

She stomps off and knocks a drink over from my table. Ice cubes and sticky liquid are all over my shoes. I try to flag down a waiter for some paper towels. I look at the song, quickly counting down; I have nothing else lined up.

0:12 seconds

0:11 seconds

0:10 seconds

Great! Just fucking great!

"We need some old school gangster rap!" the Best Man, Drew, tells me. I attempt to explain for the hundredth time about Hannah's Do Not Play List. "Fuck the Do Not Play List!" Drew yells back. And you know what? He has a valid point. So far, none of the songs I'm playing are working for this crowd. Obviously, I have an obligation to the bride; I know this it's her Big Day. But it's also counter-intuitive to play to an empty dance floor while getting hurled abuse. I have a moment of clarity and proceed to play a wild set of 90s throwback old-school rap.

- 50 Cent's "In Da Club"
- Tupac's "California Love"
- Snoop Dogg's "What's My Name?"
- Dr. Dre's "Still D.R.E."

Now that the place is finally jumping, I feel a little bit of relief. The Bridesmaids and Groomsmen lead the charge onto the floor, and for the first time since I've arrived at this wedding, I feel like I'm doing a good job—what I've been hired to do; give people a memorable night. But before I can get too comfortable, the brother-of-the-bride is back again.

"It's the second time I've requested this song!" he says, staring at me directly in the eyes, holding up two fingers a few inches from my face.

He puts both hands forcibly on the table and leans into my face. "O-Des-Za!" He shouts. "Did you forget?"

"I'm sorry, I don't know who they are?"

His anger looks so pent; his eyes are bulging out of his head.

"What do you mean you don't know who they are?" he shouts. "You're a goddamn DJ!"

Fuck this guy.

"I'm really sorry," I say. "I've never heard of them."

He shakes his head, "Then play Mumford and Sons! A lot of people want to hear it!" he demands. "It's on you if you don't play it!" he says ominously as if to threaten before abruptly turning to walk away.

"Which song?" I ask defeatedly as his back is toward me.

"You choose!" he snorts and stomps off.

I chose none.

If I'm going to have an empty dance floor, it's not going to be because of Mumford and Sons.

Three minutes later.

"Hi, my boyfriend requested a song. He says he's requested it twice, and you still haven't played it."

In retrospect, I should have quickly downloaded his songs and played them. I mean, this party was a bust anyway. Little did I know, the night was going from bad to worse.

Misha taps me on the shoulder; time for the Sparkler Exit.

As the guests file out of the room toward the sparkler exit, I can't help but feel a sense of relief.

The idea of the Sparkler Exit is to have Hannah and Eric leave the venue while all the guests are lined up on either side of the aisle, wishing them farewell, with SPARKLERS. Guests who have been drinking heavily for over six hours are being handed lit sticks of fireworks . . . this is NOT a good idea!

Misha is trying her best to hand out sparklers and keep some semblance of order, while Michael is attempting to line up the perfect shot. But the mob is unruly.

Spliffs are now being lit. Sparklers are being dropped and burning holes onto the venue's brand new red carpet. There are epic Star Wars-style sparkler battles. I smell burning hair.

Hannah is furious that her fairytale ending is not going as planned. Eric is so drunk that he's completely oblivious. And then, within a minute, they are gone. It's all over.

All the vendors kind of look at each other like we came out of the other side of battle with PTSD. We walk around shell-shocked in a daze, sweaty, exhausted, red-faced, body aching, and brains hurting.

"What just happened?" Misha and I ask each other. On paper, this was supposed to be an easy gig.

Drained, I pack up the rest of my equipment and wheel it out to my truck, trying to get home as quickly as I can. By the time I get the last of my stuff out of the restaurant, it's 1:35am, and I'm exhausted. As I load a 50-pound speaker from my trolley into the RAV, I hear the murmur of a familiar voice.

"Hey DJ . . ." Hannah's brother shouts over to me. "Total bullshit!"

Ignore it, I tell myself. You are in the home stretch. Just a few more minutes, and you are sitting in the driver's seat on your way home.

"This guy sucked," he tells his buddies standing with him. "He didn't even play my fucking songs!" he shouts to me.

Don't say anything.

Just ignore it.

It's not worth it.

You will be home soon.

My brain and common sense are trying to reason with me. Unfortunately, my mouth doesn't listen.

"Because your songs FUCKING SUCKED!" I snapped back.

Maybe it was because I was exhausted or just had had enough of this family, but I know I instantly regretted it, wishing I could rewind as I would one of my tracks, put my finger on the deck, and spin in reverse like it never happened. The downtown busy street corner became deafeningly quiet.

"What'd you just say?" he shouts over to me.

I sigh, knowing how this is going to play out. I was in the homestretch.

I had to open my big mouth.

So close.

"You got a problem?" Hannah's brother throws down his cigarette and walks toward me. His white shirt was unbuttoned, untucked, and covered in sweat.

Things escalate quickly.

"Leave him alone, Travis, you're drunk!" his girlfriend screams at him.

"Shut up bitch!" he yells at her.

"Whoa, Travis!" the Groomsman steps in front of Hannah's brother, trying to hold him back as he pushes his way toward me.

That gives me enough time to quickly throw the rest of my gear into the back of the car. Wires that are usually carefully wrapped and meticulously put away are now shoved in as quickly as I could manage as I slam the car door shut. I load the last two speakers into the back of the truck as if my life depended on it. I usually do a secondary check of the venue to make sure I haven't left any loose equipment or expensive wires behind, but not tonight. I jump in the truck and speed away.

Unharmed, although my heart is pounding and adrenaline is pumping, I pull over to the side of the road down the street to catch my breath, my hands gripping the steering wheel.

I've had this feeling before. It's nothing new. I certainly had more than my fair share of punches to the face. I was born and raised in a steel town in the 80s, after all.

CHAPTER 7

STEEL CITY

Hamilton, Ontario, Canada, was a steel town long before I was born. Often referred to as Steel City or The Hammer, Hamilton was a steel mining powerhouse, exporting 15 million tons of metal across Canada to the western United States. Stelco was founded in 1910, Dofasco shortly after, and at its peak, by the early 1940s, nearly half of Hamilton's workforce was employed in the steel industry. Everyone knew someone who worked there: a friend's dad, a guy's uncle, someone's older brother. If one of your buddies scored a shift at Stelco, it was a big deal.

It's only a 45-minute drive south of Toronto, Canada's largest city, and so it was a perfect hub to the United States. The two main factories ruled the city for over six decades. Everyone in the city had worked there, knew somebody who worked there, or was affiliated with it in some capacity. During the 80s and 90s, the money you could earn there was legendary. If an opportunity arose while you were still in high school, you dropped out, no questions asked. It happened often.

“Where’s Ricky? I haven’t seen him around school the last couple of weeks,” one of the kids would ask.

“He quit school,” another would answer. “His uncle got him a job at Stelco.”

“That lucky fucker!” we would all exclaim.

Kids our age who worked there had so much money they didn’t know what to do with it. They were buying cars, houses, and expensive clothes, while the rest of us were all drudging away in school. Ricky would pull up in front of high school a few weeks later to pick up his girlfriend in his new ride, a brand new shiny red Chevy Camaro.

I spent one single day working at Stelco. It was the hardest, nastiest, sweatiest, dirtiest, most unfulfilling work I’d ever done in my life. The foreman brought me down to a dark room beside a dormant furnace and handed me a shovel and a mask. The job was pretty straightforward:

1. Shovel a 10-foot pile of rusted steel flakes into a wheelbarrow.
2. Empty the wheelbarrow once it was full and start again.
3. Continue until the pile was done.

I dared not complain in front of the older, gruff crew that were hustling their shovels. I gritted my teeth and got down to it. It was the longest eight hours of my life. But, I had to see the day through, just to say that I had done it. Sure, the money was good, but was it worth breaking your back for? Nope! There was no way I was going to be a steelworker. Besides, music had always been my passion.

1984

I'm barely stopping to take a breath while shoveling spaghetti down my mouth.

"Slow down; there's no rush," my mom tells me from across the dinner table.

No time to talk.

"I'll be downstairs!" I shout back while leaping out of my chair, the last forkful of spaghetti hanging from my mouth.

It's my favorite time of the week. There is nowhere else I would rather be. It's Sunday, 4:57pm, and the Top 40 show on CKOC FM starts in three minutes. I ram the last forkful into my already full mouth and leap up from the dinner table. I run down the basement stairs, two steps at a time, making it to the cassette player radio with seconds to spare, flipping it on just in time.

"Welcome to the weekly Top 40!" Casey Kasem's distinctive voice announces from the boom box radio. My heart pounds with excitement. Who will be Number One this week? Will Prince's "Little Red Corvette" still be in the Top 10?"

For the next three hours, I will be glued to the radio; it's my weekly ritual.

During the countdown, I try to predict at what place my favorite songs were going to come on. The commercials seemed to last forever. Big Ed's Furniture Warehouse was having another blowout sale, and Upper James Optical was the finest in affordable men's eyewear. Boring!

Waiting, waiting, waiting . . . Casey returns.

"Coming in at Number 24 this week, from their album Combat Rock, it's The Clash with Rock The Casbah!" he informs me.

"Yes!" I exclaim; I'm giddy. I hit the large red plastic record button on the boombox.

I was an only child, raised by a single mom. So, after school, it was me and my mixtapes. But the highlight of the week was Sunday evening—CKOC's Weekly Top 40, starting at 5:00pm sharp. I'd wait, finger poised above the RECORD button, trying to anticipate the timing. I got so good I'd rarely miss the start of any song. In fact, after a while, I was a second ahead of the moment when the first notes of the song would come on. The moment my song started, I would press RECORD, then sit back and savor the feeling of knowing that song was destined to be forever in my mixtape collection.

Being an 80s kid, I made mixtapes—snippets of all my favorite songs on a Maxell 90-minute cassette. It was my prized possession, the same one I would bring to my first DJ gig at Mr. Weldon's class party. It took me almost three months to fill it up. When it snapped, I used surgical precision to repair it with Scotch tape and a pencil, using a small screwdriver to take the case apart. I'd wind the spindle and fix the delicate black film with a thin layer of tape on one side while using a small pair of fingernail scissors to cut the edges of the tape to make sure it didn't snag on the inside of the cassette cover.

It was my life. I was nine years old, and I spent every waking hour either reading comic books, playing Atari video games, watching Star Wars, or listening to music. Especially music. It was my first passion.

The first proper store-bought cassette tape I ever received was Rick James' "Street Songs" for Christmas in 1981. "Super Freak" was a huge hit at the time. I must have worn it out listening to that one song. Luckily it was the first track on the tape, so I could rewind it back to the start and play it again. I had no idea there were seven other songs on the tape.

From then on, I tightly portion-controlled my allowance money on comic books, candy, video arcades, and 45s.

Every Saturday morning, my best friend Jamie and I would walk to Limeridge Mall, making our first pitstop to Sam The Record Man. I had one of those cheap plastic turntables that were popular in the 80s, and it was starting to get a lot of use. Soon I amassed quite a collection of 80s pop hits to play on it.

- Soft Cell's "Tainted Love"
- Human League's "Don't You Want Me"
- Frankie Goes to Hollywood's "Relax"
- The Clash's "Rock the Casbah"
- Eddy Grant's "Electric Avenue"
- Van Halen's "Panama"
- Prince's "Little Red Corvette"

After we tapped the mall resources for music, bad food, and video games, we would hop on the bus to Roller Gardens, the local roller rink.

As we open the door, the musty smell of worn-in roller-skates and freshly-cooked hot dogs hits my nose. It's another Saturday afternoon at Roller Gardens.

After paying our $2 entrance fee and renting our beige roller-skates with orange wheels, we walk into the pre-teen utopia.

Roller Gardens had it all: the latest Top 40 music blasting from a massive sound system, disco lights disorientating our senses, a row of 20 video games, minimal adult supervision, disco lights flashing, loud music booming, video games in the corner, and cute girls from our class.

Roller Gardens was also another haven to hear all the latest floor fillers and roller boogie beats. Songs that weren't being played on CKOC or Casey Kasem's Top 40 could also be heard here.

- Nu Shooz's "I Can't Wait"
- Wham!'s "Wham Rap"
- Chaka Khan's "I Feel for You"
- Thompson Twins' "Love on Your Side"
- Toni Basil's "Mickey"
- Go West's "We Close Our Eyes"
- Rockwell's "Somebody's Watching Me"
- Michael Jackson's "PYT"
- Shannon's "Let The Music Play"
- Yazoo's "Situation"
- Whodini's "Freaks Come Out At Night"
- D Train's "You're The One For Me"

And when it was time to slow it down, the DJ hidden behind a glass-enclosed booth bellowed over the loudspeaker.

"OKAY, BOYS AND GIRLS, FIND A PARTNER! IT'S TIME FOR A SLOW SKATE!"

The disco ball would slow down to make the rink appear as if it were a shimmering starlight mecca. The slow song was guaranteed to be one of four songs: Spandau Ballet's "True," George Michael's "Careless Whisper," Prince's "When Doves Cry," or Madonna's "Crazy for You."

Maybe, just maybe . . . this time, I would ask one of the cute girls looking over at me to a slow skate.

Or maybe I would pop another quarter into the Street Fighter video game and play until the next fast skate came on.

When I was 11, I got the best Christmas gift ever from Uncle Doug. Doug was the quintessential young, cool uncle with great hair, a wicked sense of humor, and a knowing wink. Earlier that year, he took me for a rip around the neighborhood on his motorcycle. It was exhilarating, and I wanted to be just like him.

The tree at Grandma Janette's was decked out with silver balls and crochet angels. But this year, the shape of my present from Uncle Doug was different than the toys I usually received. I stared at the flat, wide, and thin package, the name BRENT on the tag. I could barely contain my excitement. When it was my turn, I ripped the wrapping paper from the front to reveal *Seven and The Ragged Tiger,* the latest Duran Duran record.

"Yes!" I squealed at Uncle Doug, who high-fived me.

"I thought you might like it," he said.

I spent the evening running my hand over the cover. It was so cool—Monte Carlo suits, white shoes, and bow ties. Here was a treasure map grid and a tiger eye added to the mystery. I wasn't sure what they represented but figured it must be something cool.

I knew one thing for sure: these guys had it, whatever it was. And I knew that I wanted it too. It felt a million miles away from where I lived in Hamilton.

Being born in a blue-collar town means things are a little different. It's a bit rougher around the edges and had earned a reputation to match.

DANNY AND THE CUSHION

Danny Voss was the biggest kid in class. He had long, blonde hair, freckles, and wore a jean jacket. He was tough. Rumor was his older brother was in jail. I never stood up for myself or fought back in elementary school, so I was an easy target.

While waiting in line to get back into class after lunch, my best friend, Jamie, and I were hyped up on post-lunch licorice and fizzy candy. Visibly annoyed, Danny stood in front of us with his arms crossed.

"Shut up!" he said in a low voice.

You did not mess with Danny. This was common sense at Cecil B. Stirling Elementary, but having my friends standing behind me gave me extra confidence. I uncharacteristically mouthed back.

"Why?" My heart was pounding through my shirt.

"I'll beat your head in!" was his response.

"Oh yeah," I retaliated.

"Yeah!" Danny declared loud enough for everyone to hear. "After school, you're dead meat!"

The confidence I had seconds earlier was now gone. The crowd, who had only moments ago been my supporters, had now cheered their approval for me getting my head beat in.

The post-lunch back-to-school bell rang—a deafening echo. I was terrified.

It was all the class talked about for the rest of the afternoon. Kids whispered. I would keep hearing fragments of sentences like "after school," "Danny," "beat up," and "Brent." The clock ticked away hours and minutes; it seemed like it went on forever.

At 3:00pm, as the final school bell rang, I was swarmed with the kids from class. Nobody had forgotten. I almost imagined this might be a dream.

All of the fights happened at Lions Park, the halfway point between school and home, far enough away from both teachers and parents. There were at least one or two fights a week. We were all familiar with the pattern. You walk up the hill, past the playground, and through the trees to the flat soccer field clearing at the top.

My classroom entourage of 20 kids deep followed me, like in *Rumble in The Jungle,* and I was Muhammad Ali on my way to fight George Foreman. Danny had his entourage following in front of us, constantly looking behind to make sure I was coming. My heart was pounding through my chest. With a huge lump in my throat, I couldn't swallow and thought for sure I would pee my pants.

My mind told me to run back to school as fast I could. "I forgot my homework," I would declare as I'd run in the opposite direction. But my body still walked with the herd.

Danny finally stopped at the top of the hill; the kids opened up their circle, allowing me to enter, and then closed it up. The chanting started. "Fight! Fight! Fight!" The crowd of 40 kids gathered around in a circle.

Danny came at me. The kids roared their approval. I didn't know how to fight and almost immediately surrendered. Danny started swinging, instantly connecting to my chin. I dropped like a stone. He was now sitting on top of me, hitting me all over as I covered my face.

Shots to my head and body kept coming, blow after blow. It was total carnage.

A cute blonde girl from the neighborhood had seen enough. She was a few grades older and exerted her authority, pushing her way through the crowd, and plucking me out like a cat grabbing her kitten by the scruff of the neck.

"Leave him alone, Danny!" she yelled as she grabbed my arm and dragged me out of the scrum.

I wanted to thank her, but the tears were streaming down my face.

"What are you thinking?" she scolded me. "You're not a fighter; you shouldn't be there!" She pulled me out and marched me home. She shouted at me, equal parts angry and protective. She was like the big sister I never had.

She walked me all the way to my front door. Even though I didn't say the words, I was eternally thankful, but I was too embarrassed. As soon as I stepped inside the front door, I cried my eyes out until I went to bed. I was humiliated in front of everyone.

At least Danny would know that I was a wimp, and the bullying would stop. *It's now over*, I thought to myself. He will leave me alone now.

It didn't stop . . . not even close. Danny started a new ritual that involved chasing me home after school.

When he finally found out what was going on, my step-dad, Rick, tried to intervene. Living in a townhouse complex, everyone knew where the neighborhood kids lived, and everyone definitely knew where Danny lived.

"Don't worry," he said as he pulled on his jacket. "I'm going to go talk to his parents." I knew that this was a bad idea.

"But Danny will get mad," I pleaded.

"Don't worry, I'll deal with this," he assured me as he walked out the door.

I waited anxiously for what seemed like hours. Rick was a gentle soul, an artist. Surely his calm demeanor would resolve the situation. *Adults talking to each other, what could go wrong?* I thought to myself. Rick will make everything okay.

When the door opened, Rick's face was red, and he didn't make eye contact with me. I knew then it had gone horribly wrong. He struggled to take off his jacket, tugging at the sleeve while waiting in anticipation. He crumpled it up and threw it on the closet floor. This didn't look promising. He looked at me and took a deep breath.

"What a bunch of . . ." he pauses, looking for the perfect word, "ASSHOLES!"

This was NOT good.

The next day at school, Danny let me know that he wasn't happy with Rick's visit.

"You let your parents fight your battles, wimp?" he challenged me. I stayed late at school that day and for the next few weeks, waiting until nobody was around and then taking the long way home, looking over my shoulder the entire way.

One night after dinner, Rick had another idea. He was going to teach me how to fight.

"Okay, I'm going to swing this cushion, and you're going to hit it," he said as he grabbed a soft cushion from our living room couch. Now fully armed, he told me to prepare myself. He would swing, and I would block it. I guess enough times getting hit with a cushion would numb me to Danny's fists?

"Come on, hit the cushion!" He swung it toward my face, knocking me sideways. "Harder, beat it up!"

I struggled to beat up the cushion. It never seemed to get my aggression out. Instead, I would head upstairs to my bedroom, pull out a record, put the needle on the groove, and disappear into another world. For me, that was therapy—an escape from being bullied by Danny, and maybe to take me somewhere with the cute neighborhood girl who rescued me.

Who knew that playing music would become such a big part of my life?

PICKED LAST

Mr. Adams, our gym teacher, has chosen the two team captains for our gym class Murder Ball game. Brad will captain one team and Alex the other. The remaining 16 of us line up in a row facing them so they can choose their winning team.

Brad and Alex are almost always team captains. It's a given assumption at this point. Mr. Adams likes winners. Baseball, soccer, football, basketball, it doesn't matter. They are the best athletes in class, naturally gifted at whatever sport they play. Mr. Adams treats them like gods, unlike Jamie and me. I would be surprised if he even remembered my name. Let's just say gym class is not my strong subject. I struggle to throw a football, dribble a basketball, catch a baseball, or kick a soccer ball. My report card often has comments like, "could use improvement," or "must try harder."

I can always tell who is going to get chosen first, second, or third. I've stood in this line up standing side by side with Jamie many times over the years. We get to hang out and be silly while decisions are being made as to who will go onto which team. And we have plenty of time to kill, mostly because we are always chosen last. Usually, Davey, Don, and Mike are the top three picks. They are on all of the teams. Then JJ or Ronny will get chosen next, so predictable . . .

Brad begins, "I choose Davey!" he says, pointing at Davey.

"Yes!" Davey shouts, clenching his fist in celebration and then running over to Brad and giving him a high five.

Alex goes next, "Donnie," he says confidently. Don trots over, no surprises. The roll call continues.

It gets lonely standing in line. It whittles down less and less. The new teams start to high-five each other, plan their strategies, and decide who will be in which position.

Brad and Alex are now choosing the bottom of the barrel, essentially selecting who is the least awful. It's a mere formality at this point, as their strongest players are already chosen. Now it's about picking the last of the warm bodies. I bite my lower lip. I try at sports; I really do, but it doesn't come as easily to me as music. Jamie and I are the only two left standing. Brad does a quick little "eeny-meeny-minee-moe" in his head.

"Jamie."

Jamie looks at me and gives a shrug.

With my head down and feet shuffling, I do my walk of shame, slump over to Alex's team, putting on my blue apron, ready to contribute. Maybe today will be different. Maybe today I will smash a kid with the Murder Ball. Maybe today, I will catch the ball and get one of the other teams out . . . maybe.

My mind drifts, and I start to think about my first DJ gig later that afternoon: Mr. Weldon's Valentine's Day Party.

MR. WELDON'S GRADE 5 DANCE

I turn up the collar of my stonewashed jean jacket and stare out at the faces in front of me. Ten-year-olds are a notoriously tough crowd, and even at the best of times, I don't like being the center of attention. I slip a cassette tape out of my breast pocket and slide it into the ghetto blaster.

It's the Valentine's Day Party at Cecil B. Stirling Elementary School. My Grade Five teacher, Mr. Weldon, chose me to select the music for the party. That's why I'm up here in front of the class, with a painstakingly produced mixtape in the deck and a small but growing lump in my throat. The class, hyped on homemade cupcakes and handfuls of cinnamon hearts, are totally wired, ready to go off. I take a deep gulp and push the button.

The tape hisses, then the drumbeat begins—"Too Shy" by Kajagoogoo.

This song was number eight on this week's Top 40 countdown, and it's been playing the last few Saturdays at Roller Gardens. I start bobbing my head in time with the new wave beat. I'm the DJ. The two cutest girls in the class, Terra and Joanna, stand at the back of the crowd with their crimped hair, pink halter tops with black mesh, and plastic wrist bangles just like Madonna wears.

That morning, our class exchanged Valentine's Day cards. The boys gave out He-Man and Star Wars cards, while the girls exchanged Strawberry Shortcake and Care Bears cards. I got one with a picture of

Alf, the Alien, saying: "You Are Out Of This Galaxy!" and another with Garfield the Cat saying: "Be Mine!"

The signs couldn't be clearer; this was going to be my day! As the lead singer of Kajagoogoo "whisper-sings" in a suave British accent.

♫ *Hey girl, come a little bit closer*

♫ *You're too shy, shy. Hush, hush. Eye to eye*

"Woohoo! I love this song!" Terra and Joanna shout at the top of their lungs.

Then, from the back of the room, the heckling starts. "This song sucks!" It's Rob and Andy, the Rockers of the class. Kitted out in faded Iron Maiden and Motley Crue rock t-shirts, they yell again a little bit louder in case I didn't hear it the first time.

"Brent! This song sucks! You suck!"

My face instantly turns beet red.

This is my shining moment, the perfect ending to my day. How could this be happening? Beads of sweat roll down my neck, and my jean jacket feels uncomfortably tight around my shoulders.

"Shut up, Rob!" Joanna yells.

"Yeah!" Terra confirms. "We love this song!"

But it's too late.

I see the crowd shift right before my eyes. I was losing them. Rob and Andy's taunting caught on, and soon more kids were in on it. The crowd noise gets louder, and I realize Kagagoogoo was going down in flames. The awkwardness gets too much to bear, so fighting back the tears, I push the fast-forward button. I had no choice but to end the chaos. I know there's a song on this mixtape somewhere that they like. I fast forward for a few more seconds; when I stop and press play, the sound of Quiet Riot's "Cum on Feel the Noize" blasts out of the tiny speakers. Rob and Andy shout their approval.

They like it; I'm saved! But Joanna and Terra? "Noooo!" they yell. They hate it. I look over at Mr. Weldon, who shrugs.

That was the day I learned how to read a crowd, and most importantly, how to take requests.

CHAPTER 8

REQUEST LIST

A girl with a drink in one hand and her phone in the other pushes her way through the crowd. Leaning in, she shouts over the DJ booth.

"I don't like this song; change it!"

I get this a few times at every gig. There's always that one person who hates whatever I'm playing, no matter if the dance floor is packed or not. You would think by now I'd be used to it, but it's still as irritating as it was in Grade Five.

"What song do you want?" I shout back.

"Something good . . . like Pitbull!"

"Yeah, sure," I reply. A completely vanilla request. Not a huge stretch to throw it into the mix.

"Play it next!" she demands and walks away.

I could ignore her request, but I know she will be back again if I don't, and that's more irritating.

Reading a crowd and taking requests is an art that you learn over time. There's no right or wrong answer, and every DJ is different. Some don't take any requests; they are the DJ, and they play what they want when they want. That works too. I learned that sometimes you need to give people what they want.

Having said that, there is definitely a priority Request List order. Before you take a request, you need to assess things like:

- Who are you?
- Are you a plus one or invited guest?
- Are you a bridesmaid, mother-in-law, or best man?
- Is it a good song?
- If I play it, will it clear the floor?

Seconds to spare before the song playing ends, I can find a fairly decent Pitbull song with the same tempo and quickly line it up. As the current song fades out, I mix in her request flawlessly. As expected, I don't lose any of the crowd; that's a relief. Now I should also have one complainer off my back for a while.

I look up to see Drink Girl put her drink on the table and grab her coat while chatting to her friends. She then proceeds to walk straight past me, ignoring the song, and walks out the door.

Sure, it's frustrating, but I've seen it all with requests. You name it, I've had it. I've been insulted, threatened, and even punched in the stomach for not playing a song request.

KARATE CHOP

The short girl wearing glasses had requested Taylor Swift . . . again.

"Yes, I'll play it, I promise! Just a bit later," I say, growing more frustrated.

Every time she requests Taylor Swift, she is a little bit drunker than before and gets more and more aggressive. I'm not trying to pawn her off or be patronizing; it's just that this crowd is loving the techno house vibe. To kill it now would be deadly. I may not get the floor back.

"Play my song next, or else I'll karate chop you in the stomach!" she blurts out.

"What?" I half-laugh.

"I'll hit you right in the stomach. Play it next!" She is serious. As serious as you can be while requesting Taylor Swift at a wedding while completely smashed out of your head. She stomps off and stares me down from the corner of the dance floor.

As the song's electro beats end, I realize Taylor Swift will not make the cut. I have the perfect next song lined up. The crowd will love it. Hopefully, she is too drunk to remember this time, and I can bide it over for a few songs.

The transition is immaculate; the beats sync together like they were made for each other. The crowd goes off! I lift my fingers off the mixer when something catches my attention. I turn to my left and . . .

POW!

I collapse onto the floor, winded.

“I told you!” she screams, feeling vindicated, and withdraws her fist. “That’s what happens!”

After a jolt of shock, anger quickly takes hold of me. I pull myself up and don’t say a word. I can’t speak through seeing red. I simply shoot her a look that says, *don’t ever come near me again.*

Before the next song ends, she returns, this time crying.

“I’m not really a bitch,” she sobs. They’re real tears. “I swear I’m not; I’m actually a nurse!”

I don’t know what is worse: listening to drunk crying or the pain of being hit in the stomach. It’s too much to bear. I just need this to end now. Whether it kills my dance floor or not, Taylor Swift is loaded onto the decks and, within seconds, blasts out of the speakers.

Nurse Jean Claude van Damme immediately runs onto the dance floor.

“It’s my song!” she shrieks, tears still streaming down her face.

I'M A SLAVE 4 U

The 200-person dance floor at The Columbia in New Westminster was finally in full flow after I had built it up and nourished it over the past hour. I had to drop each song from trial and error until I discovered that this crowd was all about their banging hip hop and hard rock jams. Anything else was clearing the dance floor.

The bridesmaid stumbles over and requests Selena Gomez.

"No way," I tell her. "Not that type of crowd."

"It's what the crowd wants," she hiccups. "They just don't know it yet," pointing at the full dance floor.

Sometimes when I drop a song that tanks, I quickly scribble it on the Request List. If someone on the dance floor looks at me, I shake my head, pointing to the list disapprovingly.

But not tonight. I know this crowd.

"How about some Britney Spears!" she fires back. "I have a routine to Slave 4 U; they will love it!" and starts to show me her salacious grinding routine.

Britney Spears is not even in the same universe as this crowd.

"I'm sorry, but it's not going to happen tonight," I tell her.

Wrong answer.

I could see a twitch in her eye—that twitch when you tell a drunk person something they don't want to hear. That was the moment she decided to make my life hell and proceeds to serenade me.

♫ *You suck! This song really sucks! It's so lame!*

"Listen. Honestly, I will play anything else you want other than Selena or Britney. Please, anything else, just let me know," I plead.

She storms off, and I watch as she pushes her way through the crowd. A few minutes later, the groom comes to the DJ booth with the bridesmaid standing smugly beside him.

"Hey man, can you please play her request," he's visibly annoyed. I mean, who could blame him? Discussing Britney Spears songs on your wedding day isn't exactly the top of his list. I love Britney and owe my DJ name to her unfortunate first marriage, but "I'm A Slave 4 U" hasn't packed a dance floor since 2001. But by this point, it wasn't an argument worth having. She had won. The next song I line up is her request.

Britney's sexual moans bounce out of the bass bins. Very quickly, as expected, a mass exodus occurs on the dance floor. They stare back at me like I've lost my mind. A 300-pound uncle who looks like a member of a motorcycle gang, and until seconds ago had been rocking to AC/DC, turns around and shouts, "Turn this SHIT off!"

My face burns up, red with embarrassment. The Britney-loving bridesmaid is grinding solo beside me at the DJ booth, oblivious that my work is going to be twice as difficult to get anyone to trust me again.

If there's one thing I've learned, it's that you are guaranteed to get requests, some good and some bad. But a great request at the right time can make the party. Not only does a DJ need to filter out songs, but we have a fun little game called "Translate the Song Request." It's when we need to decipher what the guest is asking for versus what the actual song is.

For example, "Hey DJ, do you have 'Small Town Girl' by Foreigner?"

The translation? The actual song is "Don't Stop Believing" by Journey, with the opening line, "Just a small town girl, living in her lonely world."

Not everybody is as OCD about song titles as me. Most guests don't know or care who it's by; they just want their song and will shout out the song lyrics over the booth until the DJ can figure it out. After a few weddings, it became a fun game, and I'm pretty good at it too.

- "Shake It Like A Polaroid" = Outkast's "Hey Ya!"
- "American Thighs" = AC/DC's "You Shook Me All Night Long"
- "It's Gonna Be A Good Night" = Black Eyed Peas' "I Gotta Feeling"
- "That Top Gun Song" = Kenny Logins' "Highway to The Danger Zone" OR The Righteous Brothers' "You've Lost That Loving Feeling"
- "Dirty Dancing Song" = Bill Medley and Jennifer Warnes "(I've Had) The Time of My Life"
- "Big Butts" = Sir Mix-A-Lot's "Baby Got Back"
- "Zodiac Sign" = Fatman Scoop's "Be Faithful"
- "Apple Bottom Jeans" = Flo Rida's "Low"
- "That Bon Jovi Song" = Bon Jovi's "Livin' on A Prayer"

I know some DJs hate getting requests, but I always figured if it takes the party to the next level, who am I to say no. In fact, sometimes it makes my job easier having fewer songs to think about.

But sometimes, getting requests just sucks. People will request a terrible song they think is good because it was a hit 10–20 years ago, but nobody wants to hear it now.

"Smooth" by Santana is definitely one of those songs that just sucks.

SMOOTH

The Lady in the Blue Dress was requesting "Smooth" by Santana, easily one of my Top DO NOT PLAYS. I've always hated the song, and every time I've attempted to play it, it ends up killing my floor.

Especially tonight, I knew it wouldn't work for this crowd. It was the final wedding after a busy patch. Once this was over, I would get a nice break for a week. I was so tired, and I couldn't wait. Tonight was going to be a piece of cake. I had done the bride's cousin's wedding, and she was also a bridesmaid at another wedding I did. I knew this crowd. Or so I thought.

For some reason, it had taken so long to get this crowd going. Maybe the bar was too far away from the dance floor, or maybe it was an older crowd, and they were not feeling it, but nothing I was dropping worked—even my sure-fire jams. In-case-of-emergency Motown classics that worked 99% of the time did nothing tonight.

After about 30 minutes, the floor was empty, and the younger crowd wanted some Top 40, Hip Hop, and Electronic, so I obliged.

Tonight I had to do my best Safecracker impersonation. Ever so patiently waiting for the right combination, the right song, the right beat to get the dance floor going. Patience is key, like breaking into a vault with my ear to the safe, turning the dial slowly.

Click - will this song work?

No

Click - will this song work?

No

Click - will this song work?

Dance floor is full.

Yes! Got it! Cracked.

Finally, I was just starting to get some traction on the floor, the groom's friends were getting their party on, and the bridesmaids were loving it. Then the Lady in the Blue Dress requested Smooth.

"No problem," I told her. "Later for sure," Later might be an hour from now or whenever the bridesmaids decided to take a break, but I was sure I could get to it as much as I hated the song.

A few songs later, she was back.

"Totally, I will play it, let me just play for these guys for a bit," I told her smiling while pointing to the now full dance floor. She wasn't happy. I got it; the music I was playing was not her cup of tea. But for the first time tonight, the floor was popping. And I would play it, just not the next song. I'd play it when I could find a good spot to transition. But this crowd was growing and getting rowdier with each song.

The third time she requested it, she was angry. She leans in, lowering her voice.

"Listen closely, we are paying for this wedding, and we want to hear Smooth," she threatens. I freeze with disbelief as she bangs her hand on the table and stomps off. Who is this person?

I've had people like her before. If they say they are paying for the wedding, I'm to instantly play their song, thereby killing the floor. There is nothing more soul-destroying than decimating your own dance floor. I had this exact scenario a few weeks earlier.

It was an obscure Akon song from 10 years ago that would not rock this crowd. I know it in my gut.

"Play this song!" he says, waving his phone in my face. He's a bit older than the rest of the guests, not dancing, just hanging out on the sidelines. A YouTube video of an Akon song from 2008 I haven't heard of is staring back at me.

"Sure man . . . later . . ." I say, pacifying him.

My obligation to tonight's bride is to make this party lit. She was at one of the most off-the-hook weddings I did last year and wanted me to repeat it for hers. Right now, the dance floor is starting to bubble. No need to jinx it with some song I haven't heard of.

A few songs later, he's back.

"YO! PLAY MY SONG BRO!" he demands.

"Soon, soon . . ." holding up my hand, hang on, dude.

I snap the headphones back over my ears and drop my head down the mixer to get out of the conversation. As soon as he walks away, I quickly jump online and download it. I'll wait for a lull in the party and drop it in to keep him happy.

Unfortunately for him, the party is starting to pop. Instead of a lull, it's gaining momentum. The groom is now on his best man's shoulders, bouncing along to the music with a circle of people around him pumping their fists and cheering.

Ten minutes later, the requester is back. His eyes are bulging out of his head, and a vein in the corner of his forehead is looking like it's about to burst.

"I'm paying for a third of this wedding!" he shouts, shoving the phone an inch away from my face.

"Okay, okay, man, chill."

He gives me a staredown as he walks away.

I don't know who he is or which third of the wedding he's paying for. The only person paying me is the bride, and she wants a rock star dance party. As expected, the dance floor dissolves as soon as his song comes on. But he's out in the middle with his wife doing some weird grinding thing. I manage about two minutes of the song before yanking it.

I don't want to repeat this tonight, so I need to find out who this Lady in the Blue Dress is. I grab the photographer who is standing nearby.

"Do you know who that Lady in the Blue Dress is?" I ask.

He rolls his eyes and tells me everything I need to know. It's the groom's aunt, one of the Vancouver elite—beyond rich. They own half the boats in the harbor and a few hundred properties around the world. People like her are not used to hearing "no" for an answer, especially not from a wedding DJ.

At this point, she has walked back to the family table where the groom's dad is sitting. The Lady in the Blue Dress speaks with great expression, waving her hands and pointing toward me. Minutes later, the dad waves to the groom as he walks by and whispers something in his ear. The groom is now approaching me.

"Hey Brent, when you get a chance, can you play my aunt's request? She's over there, the Lady in the Blue Dress . . ." the groom says.

"Yeah, I know who she is. Just that the party is finally jumping, and her request is going to kill it," I plead.

"I know, man, sorry. She's leaving soon," he offers.

It's his wedding day. He wants an easy life. He would rather be drinking with his buddies right now than discussing dance floor politics. This a low priority for him, and I'm the employee.

I shrug defeatedly and load up the song.

Santana's slinky, sexy guitar intro blasts through the speakers. As the 90s soft rock Latin hit fills the room, I can hear audible moans from my crowd. Tumbleweed descends across the floor as everyone leaves, except for the Lady in the Blue Dress and her husband. They do a sensual kind of erotic dance, just the two of them on the floor and me watching, shaking my head. When the song is over, they disappear back to the family table without even a nod in my direction.

My floor is now empty again.

The younger crowd hits the bar, never to return.

I try to mix it up with some newer music, but I've lost their trust. I lulled them in with a false sense of security and then train-wrecked it. I'm furious.

At the end of the night, I announce the last call.

The Lady in the Blue Dress approaches me to make another request. She didn't leave early after all. *I'm sure she probably could have waited 30 minutes for her song,*

This time, Nickelback.

"What do you mean you don't have any Nickelback?" she demands. "What kind of DJ are you?"

I grit my teeth; I know what I feel like saying . . .

Maybe an apology or a thank-you or maybe even a nice big tip would be nice.

If you want a song played without hesitation, for $40, I will play whatever you like . . .

$40 BLOWJOB

There are about 10 minutes or three songs until the Ugly Lights are turned on and the night is all over.

Only the true hardcore partiers are left on the dance floor. There is always a group of usual suspects that will be there until the lights are turned on. That small circle that will always shut the night down, no matter if it's 1:00am or 6:00am, they are the last ones standing.

The Best Man staggers over to the DJ booth. He's the sweatiest, drunkest guy in the room. I remove the right ear of the headphones so I can hear what he has to say.

"You taking requests . . . ?" he asks, grabbing the DJ table for support and trying to make eye contact, but he's not quite focusing, his gaze staring at the wall behind me.

"I'm almost finished; what do you want to hear?"

"TLC," he stammers.

He reaches around to his back pocket, opens his wallet, clumsily pulls out two crumpled twenties, drops them on my DJ table, and walks away.

"If you play some TLC . . ." he hiccups, "I'm guaranteed a blow job tonight . . ." he says, pointing toward one of the drunken bridesmaids.

I don't know how or why TLC would get him oral sex, but I dropped

"No Scrubs" as the next song and can only hope he had a memorable night.

For $40 I don't mind. The best is when you get a tip for a song you would have played anyway. I once got $100 for a song that I had already lined up to play next. I got pretty good at predicting what the crowd would like to hear next. When you play enough Vanilla Bangers, you get a sixth sense of what the crowd wants to hear next.

Oops, Vanilla Banger? Yeah, that's a little slang term I made up. It's an obvious or predictable bland song guaranteed to get the dance floor going. When you do this job long enough, you need a bit of slang for it all to make sense, and along the way, I made up quite a few.

BFAD LINGO

Vanilla Bangers

Obvious, predictable, or bland songs guaranteed to get the dance floor going.

"Smooth" Requests

People request a terrible song they think is good because it was a hit 10–15 years ago, but nobody wants to hear now.

Obligation Dance

When the bride or groom loves and is dancing to a particular song, guests don't want to leave them stranded, so they stay on the dance floor out of obligation even though they don't particularly like the song.

DJ Obvious

Playing the most obvious, crowd-pleasing songs to get the dance floor going.

Keepin' It Vanilla

Keeping the songs predictable and obvious throughout the night if a crowd is not adventurous.

Warm Body Gig

A gig that could be done on autopilot. You are hired to stand there, look cool, and twiddle buttons.

Uncle Ray

There's always one uncle at a wedding (usually wearing a Hawaiian shirt) that used to be a DJ and feels the need to tell me all about it.

Five-Star Killer

You kill it at a gig with a full dance floor all night and expect a 5-star review. However, an uncle or bridesmaid complains to the bride or groom that you were terrible because you didn't play their request.

Safecracker

The DJ is like a safecracker. Waiting patiently for the right combination of the right song, the right beat, or the right request to get the dance floor going.

Jigsaw Puzzle

When you have so much music, you need to fit it into a set like a jigsaw puzzle spilled onto the floor, and you need to put all the pieces put back together in the correct order.

Toothbrush Run

A toothbrush and floss kept in an emergency DJ kit used for after a meal at a wedding, and you need to run to the bathroom to get the green stuff stuck between your teeth.

Going Eazy E

Misjudging the crowd by crossing the line or going far over musically what is acceptable at a wedding. Tupac's "California Love" (Acceptable). Eazy E's "Deez Nutz" (Not Acceptable).

Deck Tease

Going over and above for the customer, with consultations, emails, and phone calls. Then through no fault of the DJ, the party is a dud, and nobody shows up.

Bathroom Buster Song

Longer songs, preferably over five minutes that you let play when you need a bathroom break.

Money Gig

Gig that you would normally turn down but you need the money.

Example: I was spinning at a Money Gig being DJ Obvious and dropping some Vanilla Bangers when I got a Smooth Request. Luckily, it was a perfect Bathroom Buster Song, so I combined it with a Toothbrush Run. When I got back, I went a bit Eazy-E on them. Uncle Ray was not impressed, I could tell he was a 5-Star Killer, so I Kept It Vanilla for the rest of the night.

FUCK HER GENTLY

This is either going to slay or completely tank, I thought to myself.

I'm sweating. There is no in-between with this one. The crowd will either think it's the best thing they have ever heard, or it will completely bomb.

The bride and groom were partiers. This I could gather from the speeches.

Before the wedding day, I was given a playlist for the party, clearly divided into early night jams for the older relatives and late-night jams for the friends. Early night offerings included the usual suspects: ABBA, Smokey Robinson, Van Morrison, Journey, Bryan Adams, and some country. The late-night list included more hip hop and raunchy songs like "Back That Azz Up" by Juvenile and "Get Low" by Lil Jon. Then tucked away at the bottom . . . "Fuck Her Gently" by Tenacious D. Tenacious D is the comedy rock band fronted by actor Jack Black.

The song is disguised as a tender ballad with X-rated lyrics. The delicate guitar strums with the main chorus about fucking softly, gently, sweetly and discreetly. I don't usually play a lot of comedy songs, so I was tentative. This is something you listen to at home . . . as a joke, right?

"I can't drop this at a wedding," I convince myself. I downloaded it anyway, just in case.

The night of the wedding was unfolding like a DJ's dream. The crowd was loving my set. Every song I dropped was killing it. The drinks were flowing, more and more people joined the dance floor as the night progressed, the crowd was going off, and it couldn't get much better. A few minutes past midnight, the bride comes up to the DJ booth.

"It's time for my song!" she says.

"Which one?" I ask.

"You know the one, 'Fuck Her Gently!'"

I'm hesitant. The dance floor has been perfectly curated over the past two hours. Why sabotage it now? Maybe she's too drunk to remember how bad the lyrics are.

"Are you sure?" I ask, looking for reassurance.

"Yep, next song!" she says definitively.

Official orders from the bride. I feel a bit better, not by much, but I slowly fade out the track playing and pick up the wireless microphone. I speak softly into the mic, a disclaimer, in case it bombs as much I think it will.

"Here's a song the bride has requested."

She grabs the microphone from my hand as I start the song.

"This is a song for the ladies, but fellas listen closely," Jack Black sings.

On cue, she sings along.

♫ *You don't always have to fuck her hard*

I quickly turn up the volume. With mic-in-hand and in her full white bridal gown, she belts out word-for-word and pitch perfectly, "*FUCK*

HER GENTLY!"

The crowd goes wild.

Like watching Cher commanding a crowd in Las Vegas, the bride nails every intonation, every hand gesture, and every filthy and hilarious lyric.

This is obviously not the first time she has sung this song in front of a crowd. The crowd is electric. This was the bride's day, and she completely owned it. I wish more brides would take note. If you want to sing "FUCK HER GENTLY" at the top of your voice on your wedding day, please do, go for it!

Even though I can gauge requests and usually play the right song at the right time, sometimes it's not about the song I play, but about the song I don't play.

GIVE A LITTLE BIT

No specific song was written on the request list; simply, *SUPERTRAMP.*

Hmmm, I like the band, but perhaps not tonight, I think to myself. It would fit nicely with some 70s rock like Fleetwood Mac, Pink Floyd, Steely Dan, but not right now. My crowd is rocking, and electro-dance-pop is hitting a sweet spot.

The sister of the groom approaches 20 minutes later. "Do you have any Supertramp?" she asks.

I was digging through my song lists. I think I had some Supertramp buried in there somewhere. "Any particular song?" I asked.

"No, just anything by Supertramp," she says, shrugging her shoulders and wandering back into the packed dance floor.

I try to figure out what song I could play. Maybe "The Logical Song" or "Goodbye Stranger" if I drop a 70s classic rock set, but why risk my dance floor for a song that may or may not work? The dance floor was bumping. In the end, I didn't bother. If she wants to hear Supertramp, she can go home and listen to it. Not tonight I have a party to rock . . .

Another relative approaches the DJ booth requesting it; I lied, telling her I didn't have any Supertramp. It seemed easier than explaining that I didn't want to play it.

At the end of the night, I was feeling on top of the world. "Another killer wedding party! Who's the man!" I say, congratulating myself and mentally patting myself on the back.

Family and friends thanked me for a great night. The step-brother of the groom approaches to shake my hand. "You did a fantastic job," he told me. A lovely guy who I was speaking with earlier in the night. I nodded my head and thanked him for sticking around until the end.

"Too bad you didn't have any Supertramp," he said.

"Strange, a few people requested it," I told him. "Do you know why? I've never had it requested before."

"You know about Jason's father, right?" he responded.

"No . . ."

I suddenly had a hollow feeling in my stomach as he told me the story of the groom's father who was no longer with us . . . and his favorite band Supertramp.

My heart sank.

There was nothing on the groom's Must Play Song List; he was so laid back and easy-going that I assumed he didn't want to burden guests with having to hear a song by a group they probably weren't familiar with. He wanted his guests to have a great time.

As I packed up my equipment, I desperately wanted to turn back the clock. Armed with this new information, it would have been so easy to throw one or two songs into the mix. I kept thinking about it for the rest of the night, but what could I do? It was over.

A few months later, I was driving to the grocery store and flipped on the radio dial to the classic rock station, half paying attention. "Give A

Little Bit" by Supertramp came on.

I signaled the car and pulled over to the side of the road.

"This is it! That's the song!" I yelled at myself. "This would have been perfect!"

Then a huge wave of guilt rolled over me, and rightly so. It's only a four-minute song! *If only I had not been so dismissive of that request. Done more homework. Asked more questions.* My ego had gotten in the way and given me one of the biggest regrets of my DJ career.

But it was also a Eureka moment.

It's not about the DJ, who is totally replaceable. It's about the audience, the guests, the crowd, the experience, and most importantly, the bride and groom. It taught me there could be good requests and bad requests, but always take them seriously.

You never know the reason why someone wants to hear a song.

CHAPTER 9

THE RING

♪♫

"Where to now?" Emma turns and looks at me with one hand on the steering wheel. I look down at the map spread out in my lap and trace our route with my finger.

"Turn right here," I say, pointing at the junction ahead. She shrugs and steers the car along the narrow road that rises up through the Yorkshire Dales. While she's got her eyes on the road, I sneak a look under the map at the backpack I've got positioned between my legs. Inside it is a water bottle, a bar of chocolate, a bottle of champagne . . . and an engagement ring.

I asked Emma if we could take a drive in the Yorkshire Dales. My plan was for us to drive and "just happen" to end up at a famous viewpoint, where I'd surprise her with an impromptu picnic and a proposal, presenting the ring and the chocolates simultaneously. By now, I knew Emma loved surprises . . . and chocolate.

"Pass over the backpack," Emma says as she adjusts the rearview mirror. "I need some water."

"Not yet!" I blurt out, sounding defensive.

"Why not?" she asks, frustration in her voice. "I'm thirsty."

Damn! I can't let her see the ring!

"I, I, I just don't want to get it out of the backpack," I reply, feeling flustered. I gesture at the road sign ahead, trying to distract her. "It's just up here," I say.

What if there's no parking? What if it's packed with tourists?

We pull into the parking area; the green hills spread out below us. As Emma maneuvers the car into the spot, I quickly pull the water bottle out of the backpack and hand it to her, zipping the bag up quickly to keep the contents a secret.

She takes the bottle. "You're weird," she says and laughs. I take a deep breath and open the door, pulling the backpack onto my shoulders. Okay, Brent, you can do this.

"Come on," I say to her, feeling confidence welling up inside of me. She smiles, grabs my hand, and follows me to the viewpoint, where I spread out the blanket and get out the strawberries and chocolate. We sit together and admire the view.

After a few minutes, I decide it's time.

"Emma," I begin, "will you marry me?"

A few heart-pounding seconds later, she mouthed the word I was waiting for.

Funny, but hundreds of years ago, Emma would have had zero say in my proposal. It would have been arranged by our families. I laugh, thinking about our parents meshing out a strategic economic alliance. Maybe I would have married Emma for some land and a couple of cows.

Thankfully, the market economy changed everything, and people no longer had to wait to inherit their parent's land. They could go out and make their own money.

Still, the concept of love and mutual attraction is still a fairly new concept, only within the last hundred years or so. Even 50 years ago, Emma might not have been able to have her own credit card or even get a job, not exactly an equal partnership. Luckily, gender-based roles went out the window in this generation, as they should.

It was only logical that gay marriage was the next step. Still, it only became legal in Canada in 2005, only the fourth country in the world to legalize it. Same-sex marriages now make up 10% of all couples.

Marriage based on respect, equality, and love. What a crazy concept.

LOVE IS LOVE

I only met them briefly, but tonight's couple, Belinda and Alyssa, seemed like they were meant to be together.

About an hour before the ceremony, I realized I was short a song!

My heart started beating through my chest, my head spinning. I didn't have the Recessional, a song that plays when the newly married couple is announced and walks back down the aisle after the ceremony. It is kind of important. I have no idea how I overlooked this; I'm usually pretty good at remembering to ask.

I reluctantly mentioned it to the wedding planner, suggesting maybe I'll use the Reception Grand Entrance Song they were going to use instead. She agreed that would work and asked if she should call the couple to double-check.

"We can't call them an hour before the ceremony!" I told her.

"Don't worry, they are chill," she reassured me. "They won't mind."

As the planner dialed the number and passed me her phone, my heart was beating through my chest. What an amateur move; I can't believe I have to bother them this close to the ceremony. When Belinda answered, I explained the situation, offering my apology and potential solution. To my surprise, they couldn't be more on board.

"Great idea, we trust you!" Belinda said.

A huge weight lifted off my shoulders.

"We can't wait to get married. See you soon!" I could hear Alyssa yell in the background. It made the entire ceremony and the rest of the day feel so relaxed. During the speeches, I found out that they were complete opposites.

- Belinda is a slob; Alyssa is a neat freak.
- Belinda likes going out; Alyssa is a homebody.
- Belinda loves to dance; Alyssa has two left feet.

As the dance party starts to ramp up, Alyssa's father approaches me to ask for the mic.

"Sorry, could I make a quick toast?" he asks.

I hand over the wireless mic and lower the music volume. He taps the microphone, and all eyes turn toward him.

"I'm sorry, everybody, I didn't mean to interrupt the party. This wasn't part of the itinerary, but I just wanted to say a few words."

Alyssa's mother, standing beside him, puts her arm around him.

"Alyssa is my little princess . . ." he starts. "She always meant the world to me. I was a very protective father when she was growing up. I only wanted the best for her, as any father would," he pauses.

Alyssa is standing in front of him in her white wedding dress. She holds both hands to her face as tears start to roll down.

"When you told me of this day and that you were getting married, I couldn't have been happier. Walking down the aisle today with you on my arm was one of the proudest moments of my life," he wipes away a tear. “There are people in this room from all over the world. From New York, Australia, Germany—they have traveled all over the world today to be here on your special day. It’s a testament to how you have changed all of our lives.” The room is silent. “Alyssa,” he looks directly at her. “I love you and wish you both all the happiness in the world. Ladies and gentlemen, please raise your glasses to the lovely couple and join me in wishing them congratulations! To Belinda and Alyssa!”

The crowd cheers, and the sound of clinking glasses fills the room.

Alyssa cries and hugs her father. Belinda joins in as the father hands me back the mic. I kind of stand there wondering how I follow this up? I quickly line up Louis Armstrong’s “What A Wonderful World,” and every single person in the room joins the dance floor.

At the end of the night, as I close the door to my truck on the empty, quiet street, both sets of parents come out of the venue and hop into a taxi waiting beside me. It’s just after 1:30am; they had stayed until the end.

The brides trail behind “Thank you so much!” they say as they take turns giving me a huge hug.

“Thanks for having me!” I tell them. “I loved being here.” And I meant it. The crowd energy was high, the dance floor didn’t stop, the requests were good, and I even got a nice tip. The night had been perfect.

A perfectly normal wedding I suppose, as it should be . . .

Much different from the first gay wedding I did back in 2010.

When I arrived to set up, it looked quieter than I expected. The chairs were prepared for the ceremony, but the entire first row of seats sat empty—seats reserved for parents, close family members, and siblings. It was supposed to be for over 100 people, but there were maybe 40 here, 15 minutes before the ceremony was due to begin.

"Great, another late start . . ." I grumble to myself. "Why can't people be on time? When the invitation says 4:00pm, it means you need to be here at 3:30, 3:45 at the latest." I'm annoyed the guests are so late because it pushes back the entire timeline for the day. Or maybe I had arrived too early. Chelsea, the wedding planner, must have given me the wrong times.

I spot her on the other side of the room, arranging the guestbook sign-in table, and walk over.

There is still hardly anybody here; there are maybe 20 people in a room that holds over 100. Is this a crowd of late arrivers? I've seen that plenty of times where the ceremony starts and someone rushes into the room loudly whispering, "Sorry I'm late," while looking for a place to sit. It's more distracting than they realize.

Then again, *maybe I'm too early,* I think to myself. I see Chelsea, the wedding planner, standing by the door. I pick up my Starbucks cup and walk over to get the scoop.

"Where is everyone? The ceremony is 5:00pm, right?" I ask Chelsea.

"Yes, some of the relatives didn't show," she tells me.

"Some?" There's hardly anybody here."

"I know some didn't approve. I know Dylan's side of the family have decided not to show," she says and shrugs.

Does she mean the ceremony, the reception, or both? The couple has been together for 13 years. They were high school sweethearts. It couldn't have been a shock to anyone.

The gift table sits empty. The buffet table is filled with food and virtually untouched. The restaurant staff and vendors, including the bartender, planner, two photographers, DJ, chef, and servers, practically outnumber the guests. I do a quick headcount: 36 people for a venue that sat 100. When they do their "thank you" speech, there is practically no one there to thank.

Ninety-year-old Grandma looks confused.

"What's going on?" she keeps asking as she is escorted to her seat by a male relative.

"It's okay, Grandma," he says while leading her with his arm.

"Why is Dylan marrying Warren?" she continues, "he should find a nice young lady . . ."

"Just have a seat, Grandma," he responds as he lowers her to her seat.

"Two boys, married? What would father think?" she continues.

What a difference a few years make. Belinda said it best during her speech years later.

"Why can't a gay couple get married and be happy . . . or miserable . . . like everyone else?"

CHAPTER 10

MY FRIENDS CALL ME DJ JACQUIE

I approach the Yaletown wine bar at 7:52pm on a Tuesday evening. I'm only a few blocks away from where I was fired a few years ago.

How times have changed, I think to myself. *Now I'm my own boss, and nobody can fire me, a* proud smile on my face as I pull open the solid glass door.

I'm a few minutes early, so I grab a seat on the leather couch near the front door.

I prefer to meet clients for a coffee. Twenty minutes is the ideal time for a consultation. It's the perfect amount of time to get to know a couple. You can get all the nitty-gritty "business" wedding talk covered and still have a few minutes for friendly chit-chat. It's also a good excuse for a follow-up. If they think of something after you leave, they can email you afterward. I've had some consultations drag on for almost an hour. That's too long. It's like a first date; you should both know pretty early if the chemistry is there or not. I can tell within seconds if they are going to book me or not.

I became fascinated with the art of conversation, studying late night-talk show hosts like Jimmy Kimmel, Jimmy Fallon, Conan O'Brien, and Craig Ferguson to see how they got the best information and conversation out of their guests. I start with the small talk and wedding chit-chat to see if we are a good fit. Then I get into my Wedding Overview, how I work, and finally, the pricing and booking procedure. I can usually time it to the minute, 20 minutes, and I'm out of there.

Tonight, Jacquie, the bride, insisted we meet up for a drink at her local wine bar, so now I'm on her turf. However, after a great phone call earlier this week, she liked me so much she booked me right then and there over the phone. She sent the deposit straight away via e-transfer and emailed back the contract within minutes. Tonight should be wrapped up quickly. It was just a mere formality to meet up and have a quick chit-chat. *This gig will be a piece of cake*, I tell myself as I order a ginger ale from the server.

As long as we can wrap this up in my usual 20 minutes, it's all good. Emma has a girl's night out, and I need to be back home by 8:45pm to put the kids to bed.

7:53pm

I'm still a few minutes early. Taking a sip of my drink, I pull out my phone to check some emails. The bar is playing some cool jazzy house vibes gently in the background.

8:05pm

Jacquie is a bit late, no problem. I'll just have to rush along with the small talk; as long as I'm out by 8:30pm, I'll be okay.

8:12pm

I order my second ginger ale.

I send Jacquie a reminder text.

Confirming our meeting, I'm at the front door on the couch.

Then one to Emma:

Client late, sorry might be late.

8:32pm

She must have bailed on me, I think to myself. I start packing up my folder and try to get the server's attention to pay for my ginger ale. We can arrange another meeting another time. I send Emma one last text to tell her the meeting was a bust when I hear a voice.

"You must be my DJ!!!"

I look up to see a fashionista straight from an episode of The Real Housewives. She has a full face of makeup and is dripping with jewelry and the tallest stilettos someone could wear without falling over. It was definitely not what I expected on the phone call. She must have recognized me from my website. I stand up, and she gives me a firm handshake. The restaurant manager is immediately by her side.

"Andréas," she coos. They hug and give each other a kiss on each cheek.

"Whatever you want izzz courtesy of the zeee house Jacquie," Andréas tells her.

She orders a bottle of sparkling wine and a tray of mussels.

"And you, sir?" he asks me.

"I'll just have another ginger ale," I say.

"Come on! Join us for a drink!" she shrieks. "It's Tuesday!"

"No, I'm good, thanks, driving," I say while making a driving motion with my hands.

"Fine, be a party pooper, more for us. Thank you, Andréas," she shoos him away. "Dan, my fiancé, will be here any second," she tells me.

Just then, in walks a scruffy good-looking dude wearing a tight Rolling Stones tongue logo t-shirt and jeans. Nothing like the Kardashian I had just met. Andréas is immediately by his side, and he orders a Budweiser. We shake hands and introduce ourselves. As I sit back down, Jacquie grabs his hand and gives him a kiss, pinching the top corner of his t-shirt. "Honey, you need to make more of an effort when we have our wedding meetings."

He nods his head at her, pulls out his phone, and starts texting. I immediately realize he has no say in this meeting. I turn my attention back to Jacquie, who is pulling out a notepad from her purse, opening it to a page filled with questions. The next 20 minutes should be interesting.

"Soooooooo," Jacquie starts the conversation. "Dan here looooooved your website!"

"Thanks!" I nod to him, and he nods back. A half-smile as he continues texting.

"Your website looks really professional," she continues. "You know Brent, I'm somewhat of a music connoisseur myself!"

"Oh yeah?" I ask. She leans in close and lowers her voice.

"My friends call me DJ Jacquie," she says, staring me directly in the eyes.

I assume she's joking.

"DJ Jacquie mixing it up on the ones and twos, WIKKA WIKKA," I laugh, making a gesture with one hand as if it's on turntables and the other hand on my ear like headphones. Jacquie is not laughing along. She is dead serious. Sweat starts to form under my armpits, my smile disappears, I let out a nervous chuckle and take a large gulp of my ginger ale.

"Whenever we have a party, and we have lots, I always select the music, isn't that right, honey?" she says while squeezing Dan's leg. He looks up from his phone and nods.

"Oh great, so what kind of music do you like?" I ask, trying to salvage the situation.

"Dan here loves the Foo Fighters and Queens of the Stone Age . . ."

"Great, so do . . ." I start. Jacquie interrupts.

"But I hate them. So, there will be none of that at my wedding. I want a wild dance party!"

"Sure, that's what I do best!" I tell her.

"But definitely nothing too current."

"Okay, maybe some old school beats, some Hip Hop . . ."

"No, I hate rap stuff."

"Motown, Disco, 90s?"

"Nope, nope, nope."

From there, she begins to reel off her list of Must Play Wedding Songs which includes mostly older songs and bands like Fleetwood Mac, Van Morrison, and some 80s music.

I do a mental facepalm. I mean, this stuff happens all the time. Why micromanage the playlist? Hire a good DJ and let them do their thing.

"Guests arrive at 7:00pm, but we want people to start dancing as soon as they come into the venue at 7:30pm," Jacquie continues. I can't help to let out a nervous laugh. Starting the dancing as soon as people walk into a room? Most would like to grab a drink and socialize as soon as they come in.

"From past experience, I find 9:00pm is usually a good time to start. It will give people a chance to grab a drink, hang up their coats, say hi . . ." She cuts me off.

"Nope. 7:30 sharp. I know this crowd, and they want to come in and party, and if you are playing good music, they won't want to grab a drink; just come straight in and hit the dance floor!"

No way, I think to myself. I've been doing this way too long to know.

"Okay, we can try . . ."

I look over at Dan as he takes a swig of his beer and checks his phone for the hundredth time. I imagine he has been dragged to every wedding consultation and been given zero input. He couldn't be less interested if he tried.

"So, you said on the phone that you have been to our venue before. Where do you usually set up your DJ spinny-stuff?" she asks.

DJs always like to set up near the bar in a smaller wedding venue. Guests can grab a drink and hit the floor with no distractions. I let her know the perfect spot that I always set up in. Guaranteed killer party spot close to the bar, tons of room for equipment and lights, lots of walkway space, and a wide-open area for a dance floor right in front. This has to be a no-brainer.

"We actually plan to set you up on the other side of the room . . . near the exit door."

A silent internal groan.

"We want people to see the mosaic tiles on the floor," she says. "If they are dancing on them, how are they going to see them? My wedding planner agrees with me."

"I see. Who is your wedding planner?" I ask. I need to salvage this meeting; maybe the wedding planner is someone I've worked with before. Sometimes they can swing if they agree with me.

"Courtney from PERFECTLY PRINCESS WEDDINGS; she's such a sweetheart."

Ugh, not Courtney! This keeps getting worse. Does she know that Jacquie is sitting here with me? She won't be happy when she finds out. She is not my biggest fan; she prefers more of the cheesy polished wedding DJ companies. I force a smile and realize this might not be such a locked-down gig after all.

"Courtney recommended I go with Hansen from GOODSPINZ." she says.

"Okay, I know Hansen," I tell her.

"Total asshole," she interrupts, "I spoke to him on the phone; we did not see eye to eye."

This is not going well. If she doesn't see eye to eye with Hansen and his crowd-pleasing antics, there is no hope for me.

I can feel the phone buzzing in my pocket. Emma is going to be late for her girl's night, and I'm stuck in this Yaletown wine bar with DJ Jacquie.

She continues to grill me for the next 20 minutes. But we were already signed and booked, so there was nothing I could do but grit my teeth and carry on. The smile from 20 minutes ago has disappeared. I can't even fake enthusiasm.

Why did I book over the phone? I agonize. The only thing left to do now was to circle her wedding date in the calendar, count down the days, and hope for the best.

The first person I see as I walk in is Courtney from PERFECTLY PRINCESS WEDDINGS—the cool kid on the wedding planner scene. We had worked together about six months prior, and it wasn't a good experience. In fact, it was a hot mess. Some wedding planners are inclusive and collaborative, but some are clipboard tyrants and enjoy ordering vendors around.

Courtney was the latter, and today, she is already starting to get on my nerves.

She stands with a clipboard in her hand, talking to her three assistants.

"Hi Courtney, sorry to interrupt . . ." I start, leaning my head in trying to get her attention.

"Oh hey, Brad was it?" she responds in a passive-aggressive tone.

I'm sure she remembers my name. The bride chose to hire me over her favorite recommendation, DJ Hansen from GOODSPINZ, and this is her way to let me know she is not impressed.

"Um, Brent . . . DJ BFAD."

"Oh, that's right, nice to see you."

I start to feel the urge to reply with something sarcastic but resist as the sweat builds under my arms.

"Quick question for you," I ask, pointing to a small three-foot table thrown in the corner. "Is this my DJ table?"

"It sure is," she says.

"Sorry, it's just a bit small for my setup. Would it be possible to get a six-foot table?"

I brought my large DJ equipment case tonight. It's made of soft metal that stores all the equipment inside, including my mixer and CDJs, so when you open it, the entire setup is ready to go. The only problem is you need a table big enough to fit it on.

"It worked for the last DJ we had here," Courtney replies. "Besides, we don't have any more six-foot tables. We used the last one for the ice sculpture," she says, pointing toward the four-foot-high meticulously carved ice swan on the other side of the room.

Ice Swan? Typical Jacquie, I thought to myself. It must have cost a few thousand dollars, more than I'm getting paid tonight.

Courtney turns her back to me and continues the conversation with her assistants without missing a beat. It's clearly her show, and I'm there to follow orders. My face instantly burns up red. Sweat gathers on my forehead. I get it. I'm not their favorite DJ, but we need to work together to make this night a success.

I'll try to keep my mouth shut. I'm a professional, after all. But this is some serious high school shit going on. I feel like I'm instantly transported into a scene from an 80s teen movie: she is one of the cool kids; I am Anthony Michael Hall from Sixteen Candles. I'm no longer a cool, mysterious DJ, but a gangly geek from a John Hughes movie.

Being part of the wedding industry is a lot like being in high school all over again. If you ever thought you were done with high school cliques after you graduated, welcome to the wedding industry. The cool kids were never a group I was associated with . . .

It's 1987, and the school bell is about to go. It's mid-morning between classes, and the narrow hallway is crammed full of loud hormonal teenagers zigzagging in every direction.

The school hallways between classes are intimidating for a Grade Nine, 14-year-old. The heavy metal girls strut down the hall in their skintight jeans, makeup, and big hair. The guys were with their peach fuzz mustaches, Iron Maiden t-shirts, and ripped jean jackets. Not only that, they all smoked cigarettes, so the rush was on for a quick puff between classes. Sir John A. Macdonald high school was a massive five floors and even had a designated smoking area.

Me? For the most part, I'm a nervous teenage wreck.

I make it to my locker. It's on the second floor around the corner from woodshop class. I can smell freshly cut wood and hear the sound of a screeching jointer saw.

I share my locker with Alfonzo. He's two years older than me and looks exactly like Jon Bon Jovi as if he was plucked from the "Livin' On A Prayer" music video. And in 1987, there was nobody else you wanted to look like as a young teenage boy than Jon Bon Jovi, with feathered long blonde hair, skintight jeans, and sunglasses permanently affixed to your head.

Alfonzo only has one book, doesn't know the locker combination, and most of the time is not at school. Every year at the school's annual Air Band competition, he would perform a Bon Jovi song and nail it. With extended hand gestures, blonde locks flowing, and girls screaming, he was as close to a rock star as Sir John A. Macdonald Secondary had.

Alfonzo was the man, and he was sharing *my* locker.

Once a week, he would ask me to bring his book to the Science class we had together. I looked forward to it. Unfortunately, being his locker buddy didn't give me too much clout in the cool department. High school was unchartered-territory; there were no rules. To make it even more confusing, now there were cliques. Nerds, Outcasts, Preppies, Cool Kids, Jocks, Cheerleaders, Skaters, Stoners . .

Not only that, a lot of cliques were dependent on what type of music you listened to. And there wasn't a lot of musical cross-genres in the 80s. You pledged allegiance with one type of music group, and then that was it. That's where you fit in socially.

- **Heavy Metal Kids:** Long hair and band t-shirts emblazoned with bands like Bon Jovi, Ratt, Whitesnake, Motley Crue, Def Leppard, Guns N' Roses, Poison, Motorhead, AC/DC, Iron Maiden, Metallica, and Van Halen.

- **Hip Hop Crew:** A fairly new genre in the 80s. Run DMC's "Raising Hell," Beastie Boys' "Licensed to Ill," LL Cool J's "I'm Bad," and Public Enemy's "It Takes A Nation of Millions" were all released in 1987.

- **Classic Rock Stoners:** The kids smoking huge spliffs before class? Yeah, they were the stoners, and they mostly had 70s rock booming from their ghetto blaster. They listened to The Doors, Led Zeppelin, Pink Floyd, and Grateful Dead.

- **Pop Crew:** If you were on the football team or a cheerleader, it was U2's "Joshua Tree," INXS' "Kick," and George Michael's "Faith" that were the big albums.

- **Goths and New Wavers:** Jeans rolled up, loafers, black mascara, black outfits, t-shirts with Goth and New Wave bands like The Cure, Jesus and Mary Chain, Depeche Mode, The Cult, New Order, and Sisters of Mercy.

- **The Dance Crew:** One of the suave lady killers in my class was a dancer, complete with a gold chain, parachute pants, and black turtleneck. I begged him to make me a mixtape of the latest dance music jams to get me up to speed. A few weeks later, during Science Class one morning, he passed me a green Sony cassette tape with the cutting dance music including breakdancing beats, electro-pop, and Latin freestyle like The Cover Girls' "Show Me."

My problem was that I was torn; I loved it all.

It was a blessing and a curse, and I couldn't pledge allegiance to any one musical style. I was a musical chameleon which made me able to socialize with all cliques. It was my survival instinct, and it served me well.

Who knew all these years later, my knowledge of all types of music would prove to be my biggest asset in the wedding DJ world? Now if only I could rock DJ Jacquie's wedding . . .

A few hours later, I get a tap on the shoulder.

"Oh, and by the way, you will need to move that speaker before dancing. The photo booth is going there," she says, pointing toward a speaker on the other side of the room.

"Wait, why didn't you tell me an hour ago while people were eating?"

"Well, if you had printed off the latest itinerary I sent you, you wouldn't have to ask me," she says, staring at the ceiling in frustration. I take a deep breath and bite my tongue; the latest itinerary was sent to me only a few hours ago . . . while I was here.

"I told Jacquie that this room flip wouldn't work," she says, exhaling loudly.

The advice I gave Jacquie was to do a flip of the room after dinner, move a few tables around here and there, putting me at the front for a better dance party location. She suggested this idea to Courtney, who told her it wouldn't work.

"It's your wedding; you're paying for it. Go for it," I told Jacquie afterward. I guess she listened to my advice because here we were. It caused Courtney extra work, and she didn't like it one bit.

"By the way, the mic sounds a bit bass-y," Courtney informs me. "Can we fix it, please?"

"Okay, I guess I can try to move the speakers now," I tell her.

"You *NEED* to stay put until you get my signal!" she scolds me like a naughty schoolboy.

Chill, Courtney, chill.

This speaker move is going to be tight. Five minutes before the last speech, I look over to Courtney, who is holding her hand up, not letting me move a minute too soon as if in protest.

"I told you not to move anything until you get my signal. Stay put until I tell you!" she repeats.

When finally given the signal, I quickly move my two speakers, stands, and cables from one end of the room to the other. I have two minutes for the turnaround. I lift the 50-pound speaker onto the stand. It's heavy, and I feel a pinch on my left index finger as I rush to put it back onto the stand.

Ahhh, damn, that hurt. Why does my finger feel wet?

I look down to see a thick steady stream of blood is running down my hand.

Perfect fucking timing!

I run to the bar, grab an unused stack of napkins off the counter, and press it onto my bloody finger. Then I head back to the DJ booth, just in time for the father-of-the-bride to conclude his speech.

". . . and, we all know, whatever my little princess wants, she gets," he says, "including the groom."

The nervous laughter in the room is palpable.

The last speech of the night was the bride and groom. After Jacquie's speech, she had scripted that she would say, "Ladies and Gentlemen, family and friends, once more, thank you for coming tonight. Now everybody, let's go crazy!"

Then I was to immediately drop Prince's "Let's Go Crazy."

In her mind, all the guests would leap out of their chairs and start to go wild on the dance floor as soon as they heard the song. Now, from personal experience, I knew this would not go down well. Rarely does something like this work when it's so contrived. Regardless, I did my job, on cue as soon as Jacquie signed off from her speech.

I'm sweating through my shirt. My throat is dry, and now the blood is dripping all down my hand; the gash is an inch across and bleeding profusely. I wrap a few clean napkins around my finger to keep it contained. The first dance is about to start in two minutes, people are gathering, and I'm still plugging in wires and moving cables off the floor. I haven't done a soundcheck. I do a Hail Mary.

"Now, everybody, let's go crazy!" Jacquie says to wrap her speech.

I start the track.

DEARLY BELOVED, WE ARE GATHERED HERE TODAY

You could almost hear the crickets coming from the crowd. I love Prince, but this was painful. The crowd does not "go crazy" as instructed. I wish

Jacquie would have let me pick a more appropriate intro to the dance party. Not even she is dancing. About halfway through, I kill it. I can't let Prince's legacy suffer through this anymore.

After playing a few of Jacquie's requests, nothing is still happening on the floor. I knew it was going to be an uphill struggle.

"Come on, BFAD!" Courtney shouts while clapping her hands as she passes the DJ booth. "Let's get it going!"

The dance floor was empty. Guests are walking by me, grabbing their coats. There were two round tables directly between me and the dance floor. It was the aunts and uncles' table; they weren't budging, so I couldn't actually see the dance floor. I couldn't read the room, so I grabbed a chair to stand on, started a track, jumping on it to see if people were responding.

"Okay, Brent, you can do this," I say, psyching myself up. "Be cool."

The trick is not to panic in situations like this, or you can make a stupid mistake. The pressure of an empty dance floor is enough to make any DJ lose their nerve. I hate a dud dance party as much as the bride and groom who are paying me.

I know this crowd and exactly what they want. Drastic times call for drastic measures. I pull out a guaranteed floor filler even though it was on Jacquie's Do Not Play List. Reading the room is vital. Anything other than that is just playing random songs you like. You may as well just plug in your Spotify playlist. Earth, Wind and Fire's "September" is dropped, and as expected, the floor starts to fill up.

Jacquie is about 10 feet away; I catch the facial expression she's making, which looks like she just ate a mouthful of sour grapes. No matter, the dance floor is filling up; her uncles and even her dad join the floor.

Okay, time to select the track, I think, looking through my trusted guaranteed wedding songs. I need another Vanilla Banger to follow this up with.

Before I can even look, the Maid-of-Honor is at the DJ booth standing in front of me.

“The Bride wants you to change this song, please,” she says.

“The dance floor is just getting started!” I plead.

“Jacquie HATES this song,” she spins around and walks away.

Damn.

I fade down after only two minutes. The crowd looks confused as I try to skillfully mix in “Brown Eyed Girl.” It sounds terrible mixed together, and the crowd is not feeling it. The floor empties as quickly as it started. Now I’m back at square one, desperately trying to find that common ground between her music list and this crowd.

One of the bride’s childhood friends is at the DJ booth. She gave a speech earlier, so she must have some clout with the bride.

“Kill the old-people music,” she laughs.

“I would love to; what would you like to hear?”

“Warren G, ‘Regulate.’”

During her speech, it seemed that she and Jacquie were practically sisters. She would know some of the bride’s secret weapons. This is perfect. I quickly mix it into the song before as it fades out.

“REGULATORS!! MOUNT UP!”

The crowd lets out a collective roar of affirmation and swarm the floor.

"Okay, I'm good for a little while." I breathe a sigh of relief; I know exactly where to go from here. I can mix in at least three or four other songs off this one.

The Maid-of-Honor is back before the song is half over, "Can you ONLY play from the bride's list, please!"

This is my last shot of injecting some energy into this party. I don't want to change the song.

"But that girl over there requested it!"

I'm desperately trying to hang onto the 90s hip-hop vibe that's going down so well.

"The Bride doesn't like this song," she gives me a look that says, *don't make me come back here again.*

Sadly, I know how this is going to end. Eyes roll as I drop yet another DJ Jacquie track. I'm stuck in DJ limbo. The worst thing is that I know I could kill it with this crowd if I could just choose my own set. The rest of the night goes on as predicted until the lights come on.

Jacquie, Courtney, and everyone else ghosts on me without saying good job, goodbye, or thank you.

It's a lonely place to be when everyone thinks the music tonight bombed, including me, who was responsible for it.

I load up my equipment while making small talk with the restaurant staff. They are polite, but I know they think I sucked. Throwing cables and wires into my bag as quickly as I can, I just want to get out of there.

As I roll out the last of my equipment, I do a Walk of Shame past the restaurant staff. They won't be referring me to any future weddings.

"Who the hell was that lame DJ?" they will ask after I leave.

Once loaded up, I sit in the driver's seat for a minute before starting the engine. I stare blankly, keys still in hand. I can't bring myself to move, reflecting on the night's events. There is still a wad of napkin stuck to my bloody finger. I tear it off, and it opens the wound again.

A slow and deliberate sigh leaves my mouth.

CHAPTER 11

YOU CAN'T CHOOSE YOUR FAMILY

I usually scan the room at a wedding and try to figure out who fits in where—a co-worker's table over there, a cousin's table over there, the parent's table over there.

Today was mostly friends and family. It was a huge Asian wedding, with over 300 people in the room at a downtown hotel. But there was one table that eluded me. And they were directly in front of the head table—prime wedding real estate.

I couldn't figure out how they fit into the picture. It was an older group who looked just like the cast of the 80s movie *Cocoon*. One guy looked exactly like the actor, Wilford Brimley—white hair, friendly smile, and a massive white mustache. There were ten of them, but they weren't mingling with the other guests, just keeping to themselves.

The groom started his speech. "I would like to thank everyone for coming today, and I would like to introduce everybody to a very special table.

Without them, I wouldn't be here," he said, pointing to the Cocoon table. "As many of you know, in the late 70s, my parents were refugees from Vietnam; this table, the Pascal family, they were our Canadian sponsors. They gave us everything for a new beginning and helped in any way they could. Everything from legal paperwork, buying groceries, and getting us on our feet in a brand new country, they were there for us."

The guests applaud as the guy who looked like Wilford Brimley smiles, stands up, and raises his hand in the air. The groom continues.

"I'm so proud to be Canadian and live in this country that has given me so much. The Pascal family is as much as my family as anyone."

They say blood is thicker than water, but many people don't know that the actual full saying is "the blood of the covenant is thicker than the water of the womb." What's mind-blowing is that this is the complete opposite meaning of the way we have come to use it. It reflects the fact that the bonds you choose for yourself can mean much more than the ones you don't have much say in.

Now somebody should have told Mother-in-Law Valerie this.

MOTHER-IN-LAW

Arman grabbed my arm as we waited in line for our coffee. His fiancé, Jazmin, and his soon-to-be-mother-in-law, Valerie, sat at a table by the window.

"I have to warn you that Valerie can be a little bit . . ." a brief pause as he searches for the correct wording, "aggressive."

I've seen it all before.

"No problem," I chuckle, attempting to assure him. I've dealt with difficult mother-in-laws before.

"No, you don't understand," he warned. "Valerie can be scary . . ." insisting I take his warning seriously.

Valerie was footing the bill for the entire wedding, so obviously, some compromises had to be made. Hey, I get it; sometimes emotions get in the way. It's nothing I can't handle.

"I just wanted to give you the heads up," he continues, "that's just her way."

"Don't worry. I will kill her with my charm," I told him. He let out a nervous chuckle as he paid for our coffees.

She was the hyper-intense, detail-orientated, "I'm reliving the wedding I never had through my daughter" mother-of-the-bride. Valerie probably married quickly and young. Now that it was her daughter's turn, she will ensure everything is perfect and exactly as it should be.

Arman and Jazmin would have happily eloped, he told me as much. The attention of the big day, the small details, and guest seating charts did not appear to be something they were particularly interested in. Hiring the DJ was an easy process. I did his friends' wedding. "Do you want to do mine?" he asked at the end of the night. The contract was signed, and we were booked. The wedding was getting close—just over a month away.

When we got back to the table with our coffees, Valerie's body language told me she was immediately confrontational, as she stared me up and down with arms crossed, leaning in. As soon as introductions and chit-chat were done, she went straight into business.

"What speakers are you bringing?"

I'm unsure how to answer. Does she want the make or model? Does she know about DJ speakers?

"I'm bringing four super loudspeakers. They have beautiful low-end frequencies that will fill the room . . ."

"We need more," she interrupts.

I take a sip of my coffee and glance over to Arman for reassurance. His gaze is firmly fixed on the edge of the table. There is no way he is getting caught up in any drama.

"Oh, I see," I start to answer, "I go to that venue often. Four speakers will be more than enough."

"It's not enough," she cuts me off before I have a chance to finish. "We like to party. You need to double that. Eight speakers."

Double? They have half the guest count of the last wedding I did there. Shifting in my seat, I swallow hard, quickly thinking about how to get out of this uncomfortable scenario.

"I could maybe rent a few more, but it would cost extra."

"What deal can you give us?" she says, staring me down with her poker face.

The contract has been signed, and the price has been agreed on with the groom. Any additional speakers would need to be charged extra. I'm not going to be out of pocket for this. I pause, searching for the right words, trying to make eye contact with the groom for support. That is the price we agreed on.

"Renting speakers are not cheap. Also, I have to drive down to pick them up and return them. Maybe an extra couple hundred dollars. I will have to look into it."

"All vendors have been giving us a deal; you need to see what you can do. Four speakers are not enough."

I look at the couple for reassurance. Arman is still staring at the floor, and the bride is texting on her phone. I guess it's just me and Mother-of-the-Bride now. I'm starting to wonder if they brought her here to haggle me down on price, a tactic to knuckle down on all the vendors and get a cheaper deal.

"I can look into it . . ."

Without missing a beat, she begins again.

"What lights are you bringing?"

"I bring lots of dancing lights. They have colors that . . ."

"How about a fog machine?"

"Uhhhh . . ."

"Lasers? You bring lasers, right?"

My price should have been doubled.

"The photographers added a video option, and the photo booth gave us two additional hours for free," she gloats. "What can you do for us?"

On and on and on it went. The barrage of negotiating and defending myself continued for another 20 minutes until the meeting was over.

As I left the coffee shop, my head was spinning. I ended up lowering my price, throwing in a bunch of extras because Valerie intimidated me, and I was trying to keep her at bay. What the hell was I thinking? I had been played.

I was angry at myself for the rest of the night. It was the last thing I thought about before bed. I hated this situation. One of the busiest weekends of the summer, and I was stuck with this mother. I knew SHE WOULD NOT be happy the day of the wedding.

That night I woke up in a cold sweat.

I look at the alarm clock beside the bed; it's 4:12 am. I try closing my eyes, but my head is spinning. How can I go on for another month with this lingering over me?

It all made sense now; I had to cancel this client.

I quietly creep out of bed and grab my laptop, propping myself up at the kitchen counter. Once the decision is made, it's one of the easiest emails I've ever written.

Hi Arman,

Thanks for meeting yesterday. I left the meeting feeling not entirely confident that I was the best fit for your wedding and will not be continuing on from this point. Apologies for the inconvenience, however, I want all my clients to feel 100% CONFIDENT with their decision to book me and felt that you still had many questions/concerns about my services.

I've contacted another DJ who is available, Hansen from GOODSPINZ, who I believe would be fantastic for your WEDDING and fit in with your vision. I'VE SENT BACK YOUR DEPOSIT and will consider our agreement void.

All the very best,

Brent

I save it as a draft. "I'll send it tomorrow," I tell myself. The next day, I don't hit the SEND button. I can't. The money is too good . . . I swallow my pride. I will suck it up for a big fat paycheck. I go back to bed and try to forget about it for the next month.

As I was set up, word was getting around the venue that the Mother-in-Law was on a rampage. One of the groomsmen approaches me.

"Have you met Valerie yet?" he asks me cautiously.

"Yes," I laugh. "All good?"

"She's been tearing a new one into everybody today!" he responds.

I was quietly hoping the coffee shop meeting with Valerie was the worst it would get; wishful thinking, I suppose. Valerie proceeded to hijack the wedding as expected. Her abrasive behavior was intimidating guests and downplaying the groom any chance she could get. Unfortunately for Arman, he was becoming a member of a family full of high achievers, including lawyers, surgeons, and academics. The bride was a doctor, and as cool of a job as it was, Arman was a professional ski instructor, which did not fit into the family social economics.

"Maybe he will one day get a REAL job," Valerie snidely comments during her speech.

Ooooooooh, nice burn, Valerie.

The crowd sort of does an uncomfortable half-laugh, unsure of her intention. She didn't even remotely crack a smile; this was no joke. And the slyly disguised remarks kept coming. It became knuckle-bitingly unwatchable.

Arman just sat there taking it; what else could he do? I can only imagine what was running through his mind; this was his new mother-in-law.

Instead of a father-daughter dance, it was no surprise that tonight we had a mother-daughter dance. A first for me, especially considering the father was alive and well, and sitting 10 feet away.

Twenty seconds into the song, Valerie steps away from her daughter and walks away back to her table. What is happening? I keep the song playing but lower the volume slightly. The bride then throws her hands in the air and walks off, also leaving. The dance floor is now empty. Everyone looks over at me.

I'm like a deer caught in the headlights. For a second, I'm not even sure if I did play the correct song. "Wait, what song does she want?" I triple-checked on the timeline; it's the correct one. Please tell me there isn't another version I should have. I can feel the sweat underneath my underarms increase.

I discreetly fade down the song to silence. The room is so uncomfortably silent I can hardly bear it. I'm not sure what to do. Seconds later, the bride runs up to the DJ booth.

"My mother has decided she doesn't like this song," she sighs. The look on her face said this wasn't the first time Valerie had pulled this kind of stunt.

"I thought this was the song I was given?" I ask.

"It is. I gave it to you, but she doesn't like it."

"What song does she want?"

"She is deciding now."

This is unbelievable. Shouldn't we have figured this out beforehand? At worst, could she not just have gone with the song I was playing? Seriously, nobody cares . . .

Soon Valerie saunters over.

"I want this song," she demands, holding up her phone. It's an old Persian song that I obviously don't have, and the internet connection at this venue is barely working.

I'm now sweating bullets. I jump on the mic to break the awkward silence. "Okay everybody, we will be right back with the mother-daughter dance . . . in just a minute . . ." my voice cracking as I speak.

Standing beside the DJ booth, both Valerie and Jazmin are ready to square up. Valerie makes the case that it's her special moment and she should get her song, but it's the final straw for Jazmin. They start to argue back and forth in Persian. It gets heated when finally Jazmin has had enough.

"It's my wedding, mother! NOT YOURS!" she screams.

The entire room is dead silent.

But I can almost feel like the room is ready to burst into applause. I hold back a grin.

"DJ, play the first song again from the start," Jazmin says and walks back to the floor, her mother following sheepishly behind.

For a second, I actually feel sorry for Valerie.

COUSIN

It's twenty minutes before the ceremony, and Beth, the bride, refuses to leave the bridal suite. I could hear the scene unfolding as I was setting up across the hall while guests made their way to the garden outside.

"Beth, everyone is waiting for you," I could hear one of the bridesmaids say.

"This is your big day, sweetie!" another chimes in.

"She doesn't want everyone looking at her," another bridesmaid is saying.

"Well, what is she going to do when she has to walk down the aisle?" another adds.

I gathered by the conversation that Beth was dreading walking down the aisle. The thought of all eyes on her was giving her a panic attack. But I already knew that Beth hated being the center of attention. During our consultation she hardly said a word. Her fiancé, Clay, did all the talking as she texted away. I barely got any eye contact for an entire hour. The conversation in the bridal room continues.

"She's going to pass out!"

"Don't freak her out; she's going to have a panic attack!"

"Give her a glass of champagne to calm her nerves."

"Do you have a spare Xanax?"

Trust me, muscle relaxants and alcohol don't mix.

Twenty minutes later, Beth makes her appearance with only minutes to spare. She is looking very loose. A vacant smile is on her face as she smiles off into the distance. Her arm is draped around her father, who is walking her down the aisle. He is practically holding her up.

To my surprise, she made it through the ceremony without a hitch. Standing outside in the rose garden in the hot sun, I thought for sure she was going to pass out.

Immediately after the ceremony, glasses of champagne are brought out on trays. The bride grabs one, knocking it back as if it were a shot. Shortly afterward, she disappears for the duration of the cocktail hour, only to reemerge at the head table for the formal sit-down dinner.

Her vacant smile an hour ago was now turning into a louder version wide-mouthed grin. It wasn't looking great, but during the speeches, it all went downhill. Between the Xanax, the champagne, and the nerves, she had lost all inhibitions.

That's when she started roasting her new in-laws as if it were a celebrity charity event.

"Clay's dad is a wimp!" she stammers. Awkward silence. You could hear a pin drop in the 200-person room. "Everyone knows he's pussy-whipped!" A gasp in the crowd.

Clay's dad, sitting only a few feet in front of her, is looking very uncomfortable. I'm trying to figure out if this is an act or if she is trying to alienate herself from her new family a mere few hours after she has become part of it.

"What?" she asks the crowd confrontationally. "Even Clay knows, he told me!"

One of the bridesmaids stands up unsure what to do, deciding if she should end the speech before Beth alienates herself from her new family more than she has. Clay, the groom, buries his head in his hands; he looks shell-shocked. His best man sitting beside him is laughing hysterically.

She kept going.;

"Clay's mom bosses everyone around; she's a you-know-what," she slurs.

This was too difficult to watch; no one was laughing. It was knuckle-bitingly cringe-inducing, even for the DJ. Please, somebody end this! I suddenly realize that I'm controlling the volume. Should I do everyone a favor and kill the mic?

Clay finally stands up; he's ushering her off of the podium.

Okay, it's finally done. She goes back to her chair and slumps down, grabs the drink from in front of her, and slams it back. Moments later, the schedule gets moved ahead, and we are into the first dance 30 minutes quicker than anticipated. She is going downhill quickly.

She can barely stand while Clay is literally holding her up.

By 9:04pm the bride is ushered into a taxicab. The groom packs up the remainder of the gifts and follows behind. Needless to say, the place clears out quickly. My job at this point wasn't to get the dance floor rocking, it was to keep the last few hangers-on mildly entertained. Within 10 minutes, the entire room is almost completely empty. It's all over.

I hadn't thought about that night again until five years later.

The ceremony is about to start in 15 minutes, and I have light classical music playing in the background as guests arrive. Shauna, the bride, is in the bridal suite with her entourage, making the final touches. One is straightening her train while another fixes her hair.

I discreetly walk over to the room and pop my head in to say, "Hi." Shauna greets me with a huge smile.

"Hi DJ, we were just talking about you!" she says.

"All good, I hope . . ." I say, laughing.

"We just realized you did my cousin's wedding a few years ago."

"Really? Who is your cousin?"

"Beth!" she says, pointing toward one of the bridesmaids.

Oh, shit, THAT Beth! From this exact room!

"Oooooh hey, Beth," I smile and give a quick wave. Beth gives a sheepish grin and turns away.

"Next time I see you, you will be married! Good luck!" I say to Shauna.

Shauna thanks me and reaches out her arms for a hug. As I go in, she whispers in my ear, "Don't worry, tonight won't be like my cousin's wedding. She's always been a nightmare."

COUSIN PT. II

The bride reluctantly admits she hired a security guard for her wedding. Her family likes to fight.

The security guard is to be stationed at the front door, just as a deterrent, of course, only getting involved if anything escalates. I mean, it couldn't be *that* bad. Surely, she is being paranoid.

Shortly after the first dance, there is already tension.

The guests are evenly divided down the side of the dance floor, about a dozen on one side and a dozen on the other. Each group is just generally talking shit, loud enough for the other side to hear.

One of the bride's cousins is wearing a black outfit complete with a black fedora hat. I have no idea why he is wearing a fedora, but he is. Cousins are always the most awkward guests; they can stick out like a sore thumb. They're not immediate family, so you may only see a cousin once every few years, but you feel obliged to invite them to your wedding.

Throughout dinner, he's getting more and more belligerent, mouthing off some of the friends. It looks like some of the guests have had enough. A small, stocky bald guy walks over to him from the right side of the dance floor and flicks the hat straight off his head.

Fedora Guy forcefully shoves the Smaller Guy onto the floor without hesitation. The Smaller Guy slides across the dance floor. He is helped up by a couple of guys who gather around him, and he's also looking very psychotic with a huge smile that indicates this may just be getting started. Any guy who gets shoved onto the ground in front of a room full of people should not be smiling.

As expected, he walks up to Fedora Guy, but instead of yelling at him or pushing him back, he sucker-punches him in the face. This is not going to end well.

Fedora Hat Guy stumbles back a few steps, takes a second to compose himself, and then lunges at the Smaller Guy. That's when the family brawl starts. Punches are thrown, and a scrum ensues. My heart is beating through my chest, pumping adrenaline, and my eyes are bulging out of my head. This is a wedding! What the hell is going on!

Only about 20 seconds have passed from the "hat flick" to an all-out brawl. It's gone from 0–100 quickly. Guests attempt to break it up, and the security guard runs into the middle, moving things out the door.

Money well spent, I have to admit.

However, aside from me, nobody in the room is phased. This obviously isn't the first wedding scrap this crowd has seen. Once the brawlers are escorted out of the room, I don't see them again for the rest of the night.

The party continues without a hitch as if nothing happened.

FATHER-IN-LAW

The father of the groom is in my face. He's upset that I haven't played his song yet. I'm not so offended; he's drunk and yelling at everyone, including the venue staff, the bartenders, the catering manager, and even his wife.

The bartenders have cut him off. We shake our heads in commiseration. This guy is single-handedly ruining the night. He is so drunk, his eyes are glazed, looking off into the distance. Oh no, here he comes again, stumbling toward me. Before I could try to look busy so I could avoid him, he loses his footing on the dance floor and stumbles backward. It's like watching an elephant tumble down full force after being shot with a dart gun. Mid fall, he catches his head on the corner of a table edge. His head bounces off, and he hits the ground with a thud so loud it could be heard over the speakers cranked at full volume.

A crowd immediately gathers around him.

After a few seconds, he sits up, propping himself with one hand, the other holding his head. As he slowly removes it, there's a pool of blood in his hand and a thick stream running down his face. He's got an open wound on the upper right side of his forehead. Within seconds, his entire face and white wedding shirt are drenched red.

Half the crowd is too drunk to register the severity of the situation. One of the waiting staff grabs a wad of paper towels from the bartender.

There is a growing pool of blood gathering on the floor. Surprisingly, his wife is screaming at him for being so drunk and messing up the party.

In all the confusion, I forget to line up the next track as the room stares in stunned silence. It's close enough to the last call at the bar; surely, the night is over. We can't continue the party with this going on. He appears to be going in and out of consciousness. Has someone called an ambulance? Is he concussed?

His wife storms up to the DJ booth, positioning herself inches from my face.

"Why are you stopping?" she screams at me. "Keep the party going!"

NEPHEW

"I Like to Move It, Move It" by Real 2 Reel is featured at every sporting event and cheesy kids' movie. *Will the crowd really be into this song?* I think to myself as the woman writes down the request.

"Do you like this song?" I ask her.

"Me? No, I hate it, but he does." She points to a 1-year-old boy running in circles on the dance floor.

I am not dropping this for a 1-year-old. My advice about kids at weddings? Leave them at home. Kids are cute. Kids at weddings are not.

There is a difference. It is a great divider of opinion, like country music, kale, or bacon. There are strong opinions for either side—you either love it or hate it—are for it or against it.

They can bring fresh energy, vital enthusiasm, and take the edge off of the day with laughter. But more often than not, they can also bring more crying fits, tantrums, spilled drinks, dirty diapers, and frustration.

Yes, ring bearers are cute with their little suits, and little flower girls are adorable with their sweet dresses, but 200 people don't want to listen to your screaming kid wearing a t-shirt that says *My Uncle Joey Is Getting Married,* or whatever.

Why waste an invite? Get a babysitter. It's selfish to think that little

Timmy is actually adding anything special to the day. Chasing the kids around, trying to get them to eat, and leaving early is not fun. Not to mention the financial cost if you are paying $100 per person, per plate, and kids are getting French fries.

Catering staff hate dealing with kids at weddings because they have to work twice as hard cleaning food and spilled drinks off the floor.

The parents leave early; they don't even stick around for the party. So, for a wedding reception with 100 people, if four are kids, you are automatically losing the four kids plus both of the parents after dinner, or eight adults. That's 12 gone from the headcount not sticking around for the party, and you are down to 88 people.

The only thing worse than kids at weddings is teenagers. They're always bored out of their minds, staring at their phones, and not bothered about your wedding.

According to one moody 14-year-old girl, I had DJ'd "the most boring party" she'd ever been to. It was a pretentious wedding at an overpriced chichi venue with a high-maintenance bride, but this was even more brutal than I thought it would be. There are also a group of 14-year-old boys in expensive-looking Armani suits with slick haircuts.

One of them keeps flashing a $100 dollar bill in my face.

"Play my song request, bro," he taunts while holding the money inches from my face.

"Which song?"

"Any of these!" he says, holding up the request list.

As expected, it's all x-rated Soundcloud mumble rap. As nice as an extra $100 would be, it's not worth veering down this slippery slope of alienating my core audience. Although I manage to play some lighter rap music, none of the teenagers dance. Instead, they slump against the wall, looking at their iPhones.

"Bro, at least play this one; everyone here knows it," he whines. I'm fairly certain nobody here knows or wants to hear "Gucci Gang" by Lil Pump, especially me. Lyrics about 'bitches doing cocaine' and 'wet pussies' aren't going to go down well and I don't want to find out.

"C'mon, man, I can't play that," I laugh.

A few songs later I notice the side of my arm is wet, I do a double take as I pat down my shirt. I look over to see nephew, he's smiling at me like a cheshire cat while holding a half empty water bottle in his hand.

"Mother fucker"

I strategically keep them at bay until the night is finished. As I'm pulling out of the parking lot, I notice the group huddled around near the exit. They shout over at me as I pass, signaling me to roll down my window. The one that was waving the $100 bill in my face yells, "Hey! Were you the DJ tonight?"

I smile and nod in his direction.

"You SUUUUUUUUUUCK!" he yells, chest puffed out with bravado he would only achieve with his posse behind him.

"Ohhhh snap!" his little friends stand behind him, hollering and high-fiving each other.

I feel like getting out of the car. "You little prick!" I grit my teeth and stop myself. Wait, what am I thinking?

Instead, I swallow my pride and push the accelerator. My paycheck from tonight is already spent, and I don't need the drama or bad review, leaving a little piece of my dignity behind as I drive away.

Sometimes when you swallow the money, it makes you choke on your pride.

"That's it! I can't do it anymore," I say, shaking my head.

Misha, the wedding planner, listens patiently. We share a quick pre-wedding coffee, and she's heard all of this before. I take another sip of coffee, searching for my next words.

"I'm done!"

She takes it in, nodding her head.

"You on your worst day is better than most wedding DJs on their best. If you weren't doing it, who would?"

Damn, it felt good to vent, but Misha was right. Whether I liked it or not, the gigs and the money kept rolling in. Who cares if I liked it or not. Sometimes you don't choose a job; a job chooses you.

It was feeding my family and paying the mortgage, and now that we had another child on the way, I guess I could suck it up for another year or so.

CHAPTER 12

CHRISTMAS PARTY

Christmas is a special time of year, a magical season filled with joy and celebration. There's nothing like celebrating the holidays surrounded by family, friends, and, of course, work colleagues.

Yes, the annual 'office party,' and the chance to share the Yuletide cheer with fellow employees. Loosen the suit-and-tie, socialize with the folks in accounting, and maybe even shake hands with the boss. It's the perfect time to let the company show you just how much they appreciate your hard work and dedication over the past year. That's the premise, anyway . . .

Sometimes, office Christmas parties can actually be fun. If the company is a cool place to work, then chances are their parties will be as well. Unfortunately, more often than not, they are more awkward than awesome, filled with disgruntled workers, unresolved office politics, and an open bar. The result can be a cringe-fest worthy of a sitcom episode, one that most people can't wait to escape.

In circumstances like this, there isn't much the DJ can do. So much of my work is reading the crowd and responding, so if people just aren't into it, then it's a tough slog. The best you can do is just do your best. Sometimes it's just not happening.

Getting over the fact that some office parties are just going to be 'boring' used to be the hardest part for me. It takes a lot out of you psychologically, trying to entice people to get up and let loose when you can tell all they want to do is get the hell out of there. I would sometimes take it personally, even though I knew I shouldn't, second-guessing myself for days afterward. *Maybe I should have played more rock anthems or less hip hop?*

But then, after one particular night, December 4th, 2014, to be exact, I swore I'd never complain about a boring party ever again.

October 14th, 2014

An email pings my inbox. I click it open immediately and scan it over.

Good morning. We are looking for a DJ for our office party at a downtown restaurant. The party starts at 6:00pm with a cocktail hour, includes a sit-down dinner, followed by dancing. Our parties usually go very late depending on how much fun everyone is having! Can you provide a quote for your services?

I look forward to hearing from you, Zara

I type a quick reply:

Hi Zara, thanks for your message. I'm available that evening, and I'd be happy to do your office party, it sounds fun!

Cheers, Brent

An hour later, the response:

That's great to hear you are available. Can you come into the office for a quick meeting later in the week? We can do the contract then.

Thanks, Zara

October 17th, 2014

I emerge from Burrard Skytrain Station and make my way to Pender Street in the heart of the financial district. It's nearly 1:00pm, and the sidewalks are packed with bankers, lawyers, and accountants finishing lunch and rushing back to their offices. I arrive at the building, head through the lobby and into the elevator, and punch the button for the eighth floor.

The door slides open. I follow the rows of doors until I find the right one and walkthrough. The secretary smiles when I tell her I'm the DJ, and I'm here to see Zara. She directs me to take a seat, then lifts the receiver of the phone.

I settle into the waiting area and look around: grey walls, beige carpet, generic financial magazines, obligatory office plants. This place is quiet and sterile—like a morgue.

I take a deep breath. I'll bet this Christmas party is going to suck, I tell myself.

Zara comes out, older, with lots of makeup, wearing a casual but expensive-looking outfit. I stand up and shake her hand. She leads me away from the reception area into a small room where I am introduced to Linda. Zara asks the questions while Linda observes silently.

There are a few questions about my style, my mood, and the vibe I would set. There are a bunch of comments about ensuring I am the "right fit" for their party. It feels strange like I am being vetted. I didn't get it. Wasn't this supposed to be at a sit-down restaurant?

Zara repeatedly stresses that this isn't a "Christmas party" but a "Holiday" party. They want to be absolutely clear that there would be No Christmas Music at All.

"I gotcha, loud and clear," I reply.

"That's great," Zara's face lights up, then she lowers her voice just slightly. "Because we really like to party."

I raise my eyebrows. *You really like to party?* I say to myself. I reply, "That's great!" though it may have sounded forced.

Linda chirps in. "Like, really . . ." her inaugural contribution to the conversation. "We really like to party."

Zara follows up, "So we want to ensure you are good to go until 1:00am."

I nod. "Yeah, sure. 1:00am, no problem. Whenever we go to is fine. I'm there till the end," I say, a nervous laugh escaping.

They look at each other and nod their heads. "That's great," Zara says. "Last year's party was epic . . . and we're hoping that this one is even better."

"Onward and upward, right?" I offer.

Zara and Linda confirm the booking. We discuss payment. They want to ensure it covers the entire night and that no overtime or extra hours would be added on at the end. I reassure them that I was committed and good to go.

"There is no way this office is going until 1:00am," I tell myself as the door closes behind me. I know parties, and this place just did not fit the bill. High-octane sales and marketing companies, software companies . . . but not this place. No chance. If my first impressions were correct, this would be wrapped by 11:00pm.

As I step into the elevator and punch the button for the lobby, a thought pops into my head: *if last year's party was so epic, why didn't they get the same DJ again?* It didn't make sense.

I think about it for a second, then the ding of the bell sounds as the doors slide open. I walk across the lobby floor, my shoes clicking on the tiles, open the doors, and wade out into the rain.

December 4th, 2014.

I had spent the afternoon crashed out on the couch, beaten down by a deathly flu. Suddenly, a reminder pops up on my phone: Zara's Party 7:00pm.

"Damn!" I curse.

"What's up?" Emma calls out from the kitchen.

"I can't do it!" I sniffle. How I'd love to lie on the couch all night, snuggled in my warm house. But the contract had been signed, and the deposit money had already been spent.

Emma walks over. "You and your man-cold," she laughs, feeling my feverish forehead. "You'll be home in bed before you know it," she says, handing me two extra-strength Tylenols and a glass of water.

I check the phone again: two hours until showtime. I peel myself off the couch and head upstairs for a hot shower. Then I climb into the car, placing the bottle of cherry cough syrup on the passenger seat, and head out into the rain.

I pull in behind a dumpster at the back of the venue and check the clock. T-90 minutes. I take another swig of the cough syrup, my hands shivering on the steering wheel and my nose running like a faucet.

The restaurant is a classic eatery, catering to the rich tourists and lunching businessmen of Vancouver. As I wheel in my gear, I pass walls decorated with awards from food magazines and black and white photos of celebrities who had dined here. It seemed an odd place for a raging party. Thankfully, the DJ booth was located beside the bathrooms, giving me ample chance to splash cold water on my face and grab handfuls of paper towels for my runny nose.

As soon as they arrive, Zara and Linda rush toward me. “We’re so excited!” they tell me.

“Yeah, me too,” I say, muffling a cough with my hand.

All too quickly, it was time to begin. I put on dinner music, ensuring there is no Christmas music on the playlist.

Dinner wraps up just before 9:00pm. “Let’s get this party started,” I mumble to myself.

I was going to have to phone this DJ set in tonight. My brain was too fuzzy to be innovative. Just play the hits, the crowd-pleasers, and keep them happy. With any luck, it would be done before 1:00am.

Suddenly, there is a flurry of activity around the coat check area. Craning my neck and squinting, I could see more than half the guests putting on their jackets, grabbing umbrellas, shaking hands, and saying goodbyes.

"What's going on?" I say to myself in disbelief. I was now staring at an almost empty room.

The remaining guests, Zara, Linda, the receptionist, the boss, and a small entourage of the usual-looking suspects, are propped up at the bar. I look closer; they are doing shots.

As I look down at the decks, a clear stream of liquid drips from my nose onto the mixer. I wipe it off with my hand and make a run to the bathroom. As I yank a towel from the dispenser, I can hear someone snorting in the cubicle behind me. Someone else with a bad cold, I guess. When the stall door opens, I notice his eyes are bulging out of his head. That must be some strong medication. He comes over and starts washing his hands.

"This cold sucks, doesn't it?" I say. He grins. "Sure thing, buddy," he says, exhaling like there's a fireball in his mouth. He pulls open the door with more force than required, banging it against the wall, and springs out. *He sure has a lot of energy,* I think to myself.

When I return, Zara is standing at the DJ booth.

"Okay," she says. "Let's start the party!"

"Now?" I ask, confused.

"Yeah," she says. "Get it rolling."

I check my phone; it's 9:17pm. This is going to be a long night.

For a DJ, there is nothing more difficult than spinning to 25 people. You need to hit a nerve with 65–70% of the group, which means I would need to play a song that at least 16 people liked—tough odds. I start second-guessing each song decision, and soon I can't stop myself. I wince as I cue up each new track; will this one bounce or bomb?

I take comfort in the fact that I was pulling from their pre-sent request list: a mix of Top 40 and Classic Rock. But it still feels awkward.

Suddenly, I feel someone standing next to me. I turn and see Snorting Bathroom Guy bouncing his head excitedly. He asks if I take song requests. I breathe a sigh of relief. At least it won't be on me if the song sucks.

"What would you like to hear?" I ask.

"'Safety Dance,'" he says, smiling like it's an inside joke.

"The 80s song?" I clarify.

"Yes!" he says while grinding his teeth. "Play it next!"

"Safety Dance," by the Canadian band Men Without Hats, is definitely *not* what I associated with a party starter. But I cue it up anyway, grateful for the pressure to be off of me. I slowly bring it in as I fade out the current track and intentionally keep the volume low in case it completely tanks.

Things escalate quickly when Leopard Print Dress Lady demands I turn the volume up.

"Louder?" I shout over the music.

She shouts back, "Yeah, DJ!" a speck of saliva hits me in the face. "Turn that shit up!" she says, smiling, a thick gob of red lipstick on her gleaming white teeth.

As if on cue, people leave the bar and start surging toward the dance floor, gyrating like teenagers on Spring Break. Within seconds, this Christmas

Holiday Party is morphing into a raging high school dance. The co-workers grind up on each other, grabbing, touching, and fondling. Then I hear the smashes. Empty glasses start to get thrown onto the wooden dance floor, spraying shards of glass everywhere. Somebody knocks into the speaker beside me; I steady it as it almost falls over—close call.

"What in the fuck is going on here?" I say to myself. I don't know if David Lynch ever directed an office Christmas Party episode of Twin Peaks, but if he did, this would be it. Was I hallucinating on cold medication?

The 80s song requests and debauchery goes on for almost an hour. I start feeling claustrophobic. I sense the walls closing in on me, like the scene from Star Wars when Luke, Leia, and Han are trapped in the garbage compactor. Suddenly, the restaurant manager appears.

"The police are on their way," he says. I raise my eyebrows.

Really? I think to myself.

"Noise complaints," he says, almost apologetically, as if this wasn't the most welcome news I'd ever heard.

"Thank you!" I blurt out and start sliding down the volume control. The crowd shouts their disapproval, but I shrug my shoulders. Zara looks furious.

Moments later, two police officers enter the restaurant and start chatting with the manager. They look surprised at how few people have managed to generate such a ruckus. One of the officers approaches me and asks me to shut it down.

"Absolutely, officer," I say. "My pleasure!"

As the police leave, Zara approaches me. "We were just getting started!" she says, visibly annoyed. "We've never had this happen before!" she says with drunken disappointment.

"Yeah, I know this sucks! Damn neighbors, trying to ruin our party . . ." I say, stopping myself before I lay it on too thick. "So um, about my payment . . ."

"Yeah . . ." she hesitates. "Let me get it from the boss . . ." she slurs and turns away.

The boss who was barely able to stand? Now I'm worried. What if they think it's my fault the party is over?

It was a long wait. I could see them discussing it. She was pointing in my direction; he was shaking his head. Eventually, she returns, handing me the check, somewhat reluctantly.

I look at the amount. There's $200 more than my fee. I look at Zara, our eyes meet, and she nods her head. Either they must have presumed I would have been rocking out until the wee hours of the morning, or the boss was too drunk to notice the amount . . . or it's a payment to keep quiet. Hush money!

I pack up with lightning speed, slam the car door, and zip out of the loading bay. I pull into my garage and don't bother to unpack; I just grab the cough syrup and head into bed.

As I drift off to sleep, I realize why they didn't get the same DJ from last year.

CHAPTER 13

SOMETIMES THINGS DON'T WORK OUT

Here we go again, another couple that hates each other. I've seen this hundreds of times before. This couple won't last; I bet on it. I've only known them for less than 10 minutes, but I can spot it a mile away.

Unfortunately, I'm caught in the crossfire.

Rebecca has grilled me for over 30 minutes about her wedding music. How she wants it played, how it should be mixed, and at what times. I bite my tongue in between sips of coffee.

At one point, Connor sheepishly pipes in.

"Honey, I'm not sure people will dance to some of your choices; maybe the DJ can help with the music."

She shoots him a look that I can only describe as daggers coming out of her eyes.

"I don't care if people dance. It's my wedding day!" she snaps.

She then turns her focus to me.

"My wedding, my music! Am I right?"

"Um, yes totally . . . your wedding . . . your music . . ." I take a deep gulp, knowing that 90% of her music will clear the dance floor. I may not be the smartest person, but I know not to cross paths with Rebecca right now.

We turn our attention to the formal music; I ask about their choice for a First Dance song.

"That John Legend song you like," Connor says. "We should use that."

"Which song?" Rebecca replies, sounding visibly annoyed.

"You know, that song that was at your brother's wedding?"

"I HATE that song," she says, rolling her eyes.

The groom turns to me and asks, "You like it, don't you?"

The energy is getting tense. I'm not even sure what to say. Where do I look? Do I take a side?

"You know that song he's talking about? You're a DJ; you definitely know it. It's terrible, right?" Rebecca demands.

"You must play it all the time. It's huge. You're the professional, what do you think?" Connor asks.

There really is no right or wrong answer.

If I agree with her, then I've lost all hope in the groom. If I agree with the groom, then I'm in the bride's bad books. It's a no-win situation. There is nothing that I can say that will make any difference. . Think about that big fat paycheck and play it like Switzerland—nice and neutral.

"Umm . . ." I nervously reply. "I'm not sure actually, I don't really have an opinion. I guess it depends on the couple."

Her eyes widen as she stares right through me. In fact, I do agree with her. I hate the song, but I can't let the groom down, so I bite my tongue. This couple is not a good fit, but who am I to say. Sometimes I scream in my head while couples exchange vows.

"Don't do it, big mistake!"

It's so obvious to me. Any vendor, including the florist, the wedding planner, and the photographer, can spot a doomed marriage a mile away. Of course, it's not in our best financial interest to dissuade a potential couple from getting married. I'm sure nobody wants to hear wedding advice from their DJ.

"You two are lovely but, have you considered maybe waiting a bit? You know, not rush into things? This is a big commitment you know . . ."

Nobody wants to call off their wedding day. I'm sure some of my couples have had this realization and still gone through with it. Like the bride who was crying most of the night. They were not happy tears either. In the middle of the dance party, she came over to say goodnight.

"You're going *now*?" I ask. I was surprised. It's her party, after all.

"Yes," she replies, her eyes red and swollen. "Thank you for your help today."

Her new husband, a chauvinistic clown, is propped up at the bar doing shots with his groomsmen. He's been ignoring her and being a jerk most of the day and now completely oblivious that his new bride is jumping into a cab alone on her way back to the hotel.

To absolutely no one's surprise, I found out that less than two years later that they got divorced. No kidding, I spotted that a mile away!

Statistically, almost half of all weddings I spin at are doomed from the beginning. 40% end in divorce, so for every 10 weddings I spin, four are doomed. Done. Over.

I wish someone would have told Connor and Rebecca. Within 10 seconds, I knew exactly how it would end.

They were complete opposites. And not in an 'opposites attract' kind of way. It was more of a 'how do you even tolerate each other?' kind of way. He was a country boy, rough around the edges, wearing a Budweiser t-shirt. She was a glamorous socialite, complete with the little pet poodle on her lap and an expensive Gucci bag over her shoulder. My best guess was this marriage had three years, max.

Everyone at the wedding knew this marriage was a bad idea. If a couple is great and easy-going, the vendors will let each other know, quite literally.

"These guys are great!"

"Yeah, I love them too; they are so nice!"

If not, we have a secret code. We talk about anything other than the couple.

"So, how are you? Nice weather today."

This was definitely a "talk about the weather" kind of couple.

During Rebecca and Connor's wedding dance party, her friends in stilettos took selfies on the dance floor and danced to Drake. I've got my music list printed beside me, complete with an X through anything resembling country or classic rock music—the Do Not Plays. Early in the night, his best man requests AC/DC.

"Sorry, man," I tell him. "It's on the Do Not Play List."

"What do you mean?" he raises an eyebrow in confusion.

"Direct order of the bride," I hold up the list. He scans the list, and his eyes widen.

"AC/DC is his favorite band," he shakes his head in disbelief. "What-A-Bitch!" It's probably not the first time he's said this out loud (maybe not even the first time he's said it to a complete stranger).

I've been so aware of "keeping the bride happy at all costs," but everyone knows this wedding is a baaaaaaaaad idea. A couple can fool their friends and family, but a wedding will show the cracks in the relationship.

Sasha was a bride that probably figured it out too late—on her wedding day.

Over a hundred of us sat in one of the swankiest expensive venues in the city, but there was one elephant in the room. Her new husband was just not that into her.

Nobody said it outright, but many of the speeches alluded to it. Every time someone mentioned the groom's love of beautiful women, Sasha knocked back another drink at the head table.

They already had a child; so I guess they decided to go through with it. Sadly, this was not the happiest day of Sasha's life. Not by a long shot.

As the evening started and the dance party got into full swing, I found she was hanging around the DJ booth more and more, asking my opinions about love, marriage, and everything else in between.

“You must have seen it all,” she slurs, clutching a Rum and Coke.

She wanted to hang out with me rather than with her friends and family. She spilled her guts about being lonely, having just moved to Vancouver, and wanted to get together with my wife, who she never met, and me. You know all that “drunk talk” that people do. I guess I was the only impartial person in the room, someone who could listen to her side of the story without judgment.

She confessed to hating his music as he danced in the middle of the floor to Backstreet Boys. In the song “Everybody (Backstreets Back),” when the singer asks, “Am I sexual?” the groom slides his hand down his chest to his waist, grabbing his crotch. His groomsmen gather in a circle around him, cheering him on.

At this point, she’s glassy-eyed, red-faced, sweaty, slurring, and stumbling. I politely speak to her while trying to rock the party for another hour. She spends more time behind the DJ booth than all my previous brides combined. If she had noticed it sooner, maybe they wouldn’t have gone through with it?

Sometimes, the wheels are set in motion, and it’s too late to put the brakes on. They are financially invested in the wedding; maybe they think it’s just “cold feet” or family pressure. There are a million reasons why couples decide to continue. I’ve had a few couples come to the realization that the wedding shouldn’t go on with a dozen or more last-minute wedding cancellations over the years.

You always remember your first wedding cancellation.

We met at a coffee shop on Main Street. During our brief consultation, her fiancé looked like he would rather be a million miles away than sitting with me discussing their "Big Day." As we sat around the three-seated table, his body language suggested he didn't want to be anywhere near her either. They appeared more like work colleagues than an engaged couple in love.

There was zero eye contact, no visible chemistry, and he was shuffling in his chair like he wanted to be anywhere but here. He couldn't care less about the wedding planning. When he did speak, he mentioned that he wanted banging house music, like a late-night rave. She wasn't as keen. I sensed as soon as they left our meeting, they probably got into an argument.

Regardless, I booked the gig. She had emailed shortly after our meeting to ask for the contract. Apparently, he had really liked me. However, I don't think I was her first choice.

A few weeks before the wedding, I get the email titled: "WEDDING CANCELLED." I quickly opened the message:

"I'm sorry to inform you that the wedding has been called off.

We will not be requiring your services."

I re-read it, trying to figure out what exactly happened. Did he walk out? Was he cheating? Did he have any intention of marrying her when we had met up at the coffee shop?

I tried to imagine the awkwardness of sending the same email to all of the other vendors. Canceled venue, canceled flowers, canceled officiant, canceled photographer. With the wedding being so close, most vendors have to keep the deposits, possibly even the full amount.

But then what's worse, calling off the wedding weeks before or actually going through with it when you know it's not going to work?

Zoey didn't even make it six months.

ZOEY, JEFF AND . . . BRYCE

Nikki, the wedding planner, is standing beside the DJ booth, asking me about any dietary restrictions for my dinner meal. I'm preoccupied, rechecking the email on my phone to make sure I have the right name.

"Who did you say referred me to the bride?" I ask.

"Zoey, one of the bridesmaids," Nikki says. "She raved about you. Said you did a wonderful job at her wedding in January!"

"Right, I thought so," reaffirming that it was the correct name.

I think I spot Zoey with a tall, handsome dude, but that definitely isn't Jeff, the groom, or is it? I do so many weddings every year, I must not even recognize him. The wedding was less than six months ago. Damn, my memory is getting foggy. Was Jeff that tall?

When Nikki takes down my food order, I head off to the bathroom to wash my hands, leaving a dinner music mix playing at low volume over the speakers.

While I reach for the soap dispenser, I see "Jeff" at the sink beside me.

"Oh, hey!" I say to him, a huge smile on my face.

"Hi," he nods, completely deadpan; it's obvious he doesn't recognize me.

"Jeff, right?" I say, still smiling.

"Uh no, Bryce . . ." he says awkwardly.

"Oh, sorry, I thought you were someone else . . ." I apologize.

Bryce? I grab a paper towel, dry my hands and head back to the DJ booth, confused. I must be mistaken. Nikki walks by, and I get her attention.

"Hey, Nikki, which one is Zoey again?" I ask.

She scans the room for a second, "Over there," she says, pointing, "the bridesmaid in the pink dress." Bryce has now returned from the bathroom. He grabs Zoey by the waist, pulls her toward him, and starts kissing her neck.

Wait, what is going on? I shake my head. The wedding was in January; it's now June. More importantly, that's Bryce, not Jeff!

This was possibly a record for the shortest wedding turnaround. Maybe one of the guests should have objected?

DOES ANYONE OBJECT?

The officiant and I compare notes before the ceremony.

"This is going to bomb badly, isn't it?" I ask her.

"Yes, it is," she tells me matter-of-factly. "I did advise strongly against this." She's nervous. It's understandable; her reputation is on the line.

However, like me, if the client is paying the bill and they want to do something radical, we have no choice. In this case, the groom was going to have a friend "object to the wedding." I mean, who were we to argue?

This was an idea that never should have gotten off the ground.

I was one of three people in the room in on the "joke," including the groom and the officiant. It was supposed to be hilarious, but we had done enough weddings to know that this was a bad idea. It's just not that funny, and more importantly, it wasn't planned out very well. It was just a random friend who the bride didn't know, not a professional actor. Something on this scale needs to be rehearsed and practiced many times to get it right.

In the movies, that's where everyone in the audience gasps, trying to figure out what is going on. There is always disruption and panic! This was quite the opposite. It was embarrassing to witness. I wanted to crawl into a hole until it was over. I can't imagine how the bride felt.

"Does anybody object to this wedding?" Carol, the officiant, asks the guests.

A guy at the back of the room hesitantly strolls down the aisle.

"I do!" he says softly, and his voice cracks. Some older people at the front of the aisle don't even hear what he says. He was obviously nervous and messed up as expected.

As unique as a ceremony should be, it also needs to be accessible and follow some formal cues. It's easy enough for the guests to follow along as well as cover certain criteria including vows, rings, and the big kiss at the end.

Carol was my favorite officiant. You could set your watch to her ceremonies. They worked like clockwork, which made my life as a DJ easy. I always knew exactly when to cue the music. When the couple was going to sign their paperwork, I had the music ready. When they recessed after the ceremony, I knew the exact cue. We had worked together so many times. I had her ceremony down to the minute.

Eighteen minutes.

One minute: The Intro. "Welcome, ladies and gentlemen!"

Four minutes: The Rings. "Now it's time to exchange the rings."

Four minutes: The Vows. "The bride and groom have a few words to say to each other."

Two minutes: The Kiss. "You may now kiss the bride!"

Four minutes: Registry signing for four minutes while I play soft background music.

Two minutes: The Final Words. The couple goes back up to the front.

"Please welcome for the first time (insert bride and groom name)!"

One minute: The Recessional. I play upbeat music while they exit. It's easy and stress-free every single time.

When I worked with Jerry, the officiant, it was never the same way each time. I never knew what he was going to say. He looked like a mix between Santa Claus and Colonel Sanders, always smiling and in a good mood, but his timekeeping was pretty loose.

In real life, people can adapt accordingly, but when the entire day is resting on your words, it can make for a tense situation—the bride and groom on pins and needles wondering if he would show up at all. He was always rolling in less than ten minutes before the ceremony, reeking of alcohol and stale cigarettes.

"Do you think he will show up? Should we call him?"

"Don't worry, I know Jerry, he'll be late, but he'll be here!" he was always there.

Post-ceremony, when champagne is passed, he always grabs two off the tray as it makes his way to him. One for me and one for him, but I don't drink champagne, so he would keep both.

"Oh, if I must, just a little sip," he looks at me and winks.

He was also a businessman, sometimes cramming four or five weddings into a single day all over the city. It's common knowledge that most weddings run late, so he was almost always running behind playing catch up. Another problem when you are doing that many weddings is that you may forget a name here or there. Again, in real life, it's not a problem. But when you have hundreds of people hanging on your every word, it can be awkward or uncomfortable at best.

"Okay, I just need to gather my thoughts. The last wedding ran late, and the traffic was terrible. Remind me the couple's names . . ." he asks.

Unlike the officiants who have no choice, I never say the bride and groom's names on the mic. Unless I have it written down in front of me, I won't dare say their first names on the mic. To me, they are "bride and groom" all night. There is always a risk you can get it wrong, so when I get on the mic to announce the grand entrance, it's always, "Ladies and gentlemen, please welcome the BRIDE AND GROOM!" or "Congrats to the BRIDE AND GROOM!"

"Please welcome for the first time, Tara and Blake!" I announce. The room is silent. That half-a-second of self-doubt creeps in. Why is nobody applauding?

A voice shouts from the back of the room—one of the older aunts, "It's Kara, you jackass!" The room breaks out in laughter at my expense. A little bead of sweat forms on my forehead as I laugh it off and re-announce it properly.

"Yes, of course, I meant Kara and Blake, please give it up!" the crowd cheers, still laughing. As they walk in, the bride shoots me a quick evil look.

But nothing is ever as bad as when the officiant does it. I've seen this many times. They will call the bride the bridesmaid's name, and the groom and the best man's name, and get it wrong. This happens more often than you would think. Maybe one out of 20 weddings. Most of the time, it's laughed off. Brad, Heather, Sarah—after a while, they all sound so similar.

Today's bride was named Siobhan (pronounced Shi-VAWN), and Jerry was struggling.

"Welcome everyone to the wedding of *SIBBBBIN* . . . and Corey!" he starts the ceremony.

The audience let out a collective laugh. Whoooo, an ice breaker, a great start to the wedding, Jerry. It breaks the tension. The bride and groom chuckle. Jerry apologizes and carries on.

"Sorry about that . . ." he says, promising to get it right next time.

Unfortunately, the second time is a swing and a miss: *SHIVEEEEEN.*

One person at the back shouts out her correct name.

Third time: SAAAABON.

Nobody laughs. People start getting visibly irritated. It's knuckle-bitingly cringe-inducing.

After a fourth time and fifth time, he gets it wrong again. He's flustered and tries to joke it off by calling her "What's Her Name," but it doesn't connect with the audience. It's no longer funny, and it's unbearable to watch.

It ended with him flubbing the names until the bitter end. I guess he was having a bad day at work. I could totally relate.

BUTTERFLIES

Do you ever get butterflies in your stomach before work? Getting out of bed is the hardest thing in the world, and the thought of facing another day is a total drag.

What's even worse than that? If you are hired to be the life of the party, and you hate everything about your job.

For me, it was the music, the drunk guests, the sleepless nights, the setting up, the other vendors, the food, the load-ins, the lights, the kids, the bad requests, the vomit, and the mother-in-laws—I could do without them

Maybe it's time for a regular job again, I would start telling myself before every gig.

Mentally, I was done, but financially, I still had skin in the game. For a couple of days a week, I was able to pay my mortgage and bills, put food on the table, and afford to go on holidays with the family.

But it was a Faustian Bargain. I was as busy as I could possibly be, charging the highest price for a wedding DJ that I could be, but it was definitely taking its toll on my mental and physical health. You can only manage to crawl into bed at 4:00am, only to be woken up at 7:00am so often, but I needed to do it. It was my only source of income, and the money was just too good. But I may as well have been back at an office job, punching the clock to take home a sweet paycheck.

Only, you can't exactly call in sick for a wedding . . .

28 MINUTES

I'm curled up in the fetal position on the bedroom floor.

The slightest movement increases the danger of me violently throwing up. Carefully, I crane my neck without moving the rest of my body to read the digital alarm clock on top of the dresser. The red neon glowing numbers flash.

3:02pm

I have to leave for work in 28 minutes.

The sickness started mid-morning, sometime after breakfast. Now I've been frozen solid for the past hour on the floor wearing nothing but a t-shirt, wondering how this happened. Was it the curry we had last night? Food poisoning? Why wasn't Emma sick? Maybe I got that mystery stomach bug from Samuel, but he got rid of that last week. A couple of neighbors also had it—a 24-hour thing.

Either way, I have no idea how I'm going to make it to the toilet again to throw up, let alone to the wedding that starts in three hours. I need to leave at 3:30pm if I'm going to make it on time. The countdown begins.

3:04pm

I'm tight, afraid to move a muscle, and trying to keep a balance between tenseness and relaxation. Once I relax too much, that horrible feeling in my stomach starts again. I have a terrible feeling that this isn't going to pass anytime soon.

I need to change my mindset if anything is going to happen. I need to push through with mental strength. Carefully, I devise my escape from the bedroom floor in my head, and with military precision, I review all the step-by-step details.

1. Quick ice-cold shower.
2. No deodorant, skin cream, or hair gel. The smell might make me sick.
3. Mouthwash only. Toothbrush and toothpaste will make me gag.
4. Pack some bathroom supplies: mouthwash, Pepto-Bismol, and extra-strength Tylenol.
5. Pick out clothes to wear, preferably an older outfit: a dress shirt, a pair of pants, and a spare pair of boxers.
6. Pack for the car ride: water, towels, and a bucket.

Once I have visualized every detail in my head, I plan my route to the venue: take all of the back roads in case I need to pull over and drive slowly as the motion of the car might make me sick. I check the clock one more time.

3:12pm

Today of all days, the wedding is at Chez Bleu Restaurant, a restaurant that is more prestigious, more exclusive, more expensive, swankier, and snobbier than any other in the city. It also has the most complicated setup. I need to park around the corner and wheel my equipment down an uneven cobblestone path. I have to be at the venue at 4:00pm sharp as guests arrive in the room at 6:00pm for the reception. This gives me two hours to load in, set up, and park.

I've always had paranoia for timekeeping. It's one of the only things I'm super obsessive about. I hate being late, and I hate when people are late for me. Getting to this gig on time was part of who I was. Whether I'm sick or not didn't matter, it's irrelevant. I will be there on time. It's a part of my DNA.

The couple certainly doesn't care if I'm sick or not. They just want me there on time to DJ. They booked me almost a year ago for their special day, but for me, it's just another day, and today just happened to be a sick day.

I have a friend who is a surgeon. We once had a conversation about the similarities of our jobs. Not that surgery and DJing are in the same category, except that we both can't have an "off" day. His patients are going under the knife, and my wedding couples don't care if we've had no sleep, have been up all night with the kids, are tired and grumpy, or have a stomach bug. We've been hired to do one job: show up and perform. As soon as we arrive at work, we need to be "on" and do whatever it takes. The surgeon must perform surgery with precise perfection, and I bring the party. Sick as a dog or not, I had to turn that switch . . .

3:15pm

It's now or never.

I pull myself up and head to the shower. It's only seven footsteps away from where I was curled up, but it feels miles away. With my stomach turning and head pounding, I turn on the cold water. Hopefully, this will bring me back to life. Step one is complete.

3:21pm

Steps two and three go exactly according to plan. Although, if any of the guests come within two feet of me, they will get a godawful stench of green smoke coming out of my mouth. My unshaven face and lack of deodorant only add to my sickly appearance.

Roadblock at step four.

We are all out of Pepto-Bismol. I thought we had a spare bottle in case of emergencies, but it must have been used up during my last few weddings to calm my nerves. This inevitably affects my drive to the venue as I will need to find a drug store on the way. But this can be turned to my advantage in case there are any other supplies that I need to pick up.

3:22pm

Step five: getting dressed.

My first choice is a crisp blue Ben Sherman checkered button-down shirt and perfectly fitted black trousers, but I can't risk permanent staining on my favorite outfit. The second choice isn't so bad, but it's been a while since I've worn it, and it's wrinkly. No time to iron. Must move on.

3:23pm

Step six: spare pair of boxers. Make that two spare pairs of boxers, just in case.

3:24pm

Backpack full of supplies. I grasp the handrail and head downstairs to the garage.

3:25pm

Luckily the RAV was still packed up from my last gig, so no heavy lifting was required. Sliding into the driver seat, I pull my laptop open, making sure I have all of my music and special songs ready to go, triple checking everything: the Grand Entrance Song, the First Dance, the Father-Daughter Dance, the Mother-Son Dance, the Cake Cutting Song, the Bouquet, and Garter songs, as well as their special music for dinner and dancing.

I close the laptop, putting it on the passenger's seat, and start the ignition.

3:30pm

I hesitantly shift the gear into the drive position.

THE HUGGER AND THE MAGICIAN

It's amazing what fresh air, a bottle of Pepto Bismol, a handful of Extra Strength Tylenol and some adrenaline can do. By 6:00pm, I was feeling semi-normal. Obviously, I would rather be at home curled up in bed, but tonight I would push through. *Yeah, I might just make it,* I thought to myself. That was until the groom got his hands on me.

Ivan hugs me so hard it hurts; I'm sure I have bruises on my arms.

His firm "man hug" catches me off guard, and I try to reciprocate, but my arms are pinned to my sides. I feel like a little kid being smothered by his overly affectionate uncle. He's the same height as me but with a stocky build. When we shook hands earlier in the night, his hands, twice the size of mine, engulfed mine like oven mitts. I felt like a 6-year-old shaking an adult's hand.

It's unexpected, although not unwelcome. I mean, it's the happiest day of his life, after all, and he's loving every minute of it.

Post-hug, I'm thrilled he's so happy. It takes away a level of pressure, and I feel more relaxed behind the decks. We are less than an hour into the dance party, which confirms I'm doing a good job in his eyes. Instinctively, it makes me want to take the party to the next level.

Groomsmen request some old-school hip hop. Done!

Bridesmaids request some 90s boy bands. Done!

The bride wants the Calvin Harris and Rihanna song. Done!

Things are popping, and the dance party is covering every inch of the small room at the Chez Bleu Restaurant. Some of the guys are outside smoking cigars, the strong smell wafting in brings me back to my own wedding 13 years ago in Havana, Cuba. Ivan is dancing, arms around his best friends; the vibe is amazing. He comes back over to the DJ booth, sweat dripping down his forehead.

"Thanks for coming out tonight. You are killing it," he says with a big smile.

"Thanks for having me," I reply.

"Come on! We're doing shots. Have one with me!"

I decline with a laugh.

"Okay, man, thanks again for everything. This is so great," and with that, he comes in for another hug. A tight squeeze that feels like I'm being wrapped up in a warm blanket.

He eventually returns to the DJ booth every 15 minutes to give another hug. After a while, I start to anticipate them. It's the first job I've had where this is an acceptable form of appreciation. When was the last time you got a hug at work? I could never have imagined that while I worked in the software industry all those years.

"Hey Brent, you did a great job on that report; those spreadsheets were top notch. Come and give me a hug!"

Finally, it's the last song of the night—a 1:00am finish. That's the golden hour to wrap things up. And I wrapped it up beautifully. The last song of the night is a request from Ivan: Aerosmith's "I Don't Wanna Miss a Thing," a group-circle-singalong. Shouting the chorus until the very last second, I add a nifty echo effect and fade it out. Music down, strobe lights off. Bam, the perfect finish!

"Thanks, guys, good night! Get home safe!" I shout into the microphone.

The house lights are still off, and the room is completely dark. Nobody is even attempting to leave.

Eventually, they start the chant, "BEEEFAD! BEEEFAD!" so I line up one more song.

One of the servers brushes past me with a tray full of empty drinks, so I get her attention, "Hey, do you mind turning on the house lights now?" I ask her. Once the Ugly Lights are on, this crowd will be filing out the exit.

"We're here until 2:00am," she says while continuing to walk past. "I guess that means you too."

My contract specifically says a 1:00am finish.

"No . . . I'm actually done now," I say as she walks away.

The next song is playing in the background, and I jog over to the bar.

"Feel free to crank up the house lights," I mention to the bartender.

He shakes his head, "Sorry mate, we're here until 2:00am."

What is going on here? I think to myself. Most venues are happy to turn up the lights at the end of the night. Ugly Lights up, people leave, and everyone gets to go home. Simple. Nobody wants to hang around longer than they need to. I'm done, but as long as the house lights are on, people are standing in the dark yelling at me.

Contracts with end times are fine when everyone is stone-cold sober, sitting around being polite. It's quite a different thing when everyone is hammered at 1:00am. I speak to the groom, but he is completely wasted.

"Keep going, man!" he says, grabbing my shoulder. "You are killing it!"

"Sorry, Ivan, I'm done."

Normally, I wouldn't mind sticking around for a bit, but I still feel sick as a dog. Also, when I booked this gig, I gave a huge discount. I think Ivan got more than his money's worth tonight. There are now only about 15 people left. I'm not playing for another hour unless he's willing to pay overtime, but they hardly ever do.

After dinner, I overhear the photographer and wedding planner talking about staying an additional two hours of overtime. "Sure, I charge $300 an hour overtime," she says without hesitation.

I'm in the wrong job, I think to myself, and throw on a few random songs to keep them happy.

There is a closet area behind me where my stuff is stored. I open the door and start gathering my things. I'm getting ready to shut it down when I turn around and am face-to-face with the restaurant manager, Jacob.

"Don't you ever tell my employees what to do!" he whispers low to me, his face red, fists clenched.

"Wait, what?" I reply, completely shocked.

"We are here until 2:00am, so are you!"

"Hey, I think you got the wrong end of the stick," I tell him.

He gets closer, almost nose-to-nose, giving me a stare-down.

"You keep playing!"

"Whoa, back up!" I tell him as I'm shaking with frustration. I feel like I'm back at elementary school getting bullied by Danny Voss.

I'm hired by the bride and groom, not this guy.

Five-star hotels and eating establishments seem to be breeding grounds for such entitled employee behavior. It's almost expected. The staff has to put up with these psychos for a healthy paycheck. What happens with a server who spills a drink? Or forgets an order? Or mixes up an important table?

I play for a few more songs and intentionally tank, playing a few bad songs in a row so I can pack up. The remaining few are too drunk to notice. Jacob gives me an evil glare as I leave the room.

As I wheel my equipment out onto the sidewalk outside the restaurant, Ivan is with his crew laughing and smoking cigars. He notices me coming out, calls me over, grabs me by the shoulders, and gives one more enormous hug.

Saved the best for last.

But you know what they say, keep your friends close and your enemies closer.

A few days after Chez Bleu and the Jacob incident, the phone rang. A number I didn't recognize.

"Is this DJ BFAD?" the voice on the other end asks.

"Yes, speaking," I answer, expecting it to be a new client inquiry.

"Hey, this is Seymour! I own Seymour Sound, or as I like to say, Seymour Sound, the biggest DJ company in town!" he says, laughing at his own joke.

"Oh, hi," I answer. Maybe he's looking to add another DJ to his team.

"I'm sure you've heard of my company around town," he continues to force-feed me information. "On any given Saturday, I got up to 20 guys out rocking weddings all over the city!"

"Wow, that's awesome, Seymour," I reply. I had never heard of him.

"Anyway, the reason for my call is that me and some of the 'real' wedding DJs in town have a little monthly get-together," he pauses, "and I would like to invite you."

More connections, more contacts, widen my DJ circle. It sounded good.

"Thanks, Seymour."

"See you next Wednesday night eight at the Railway Club downtown."

This should be great; I've been invited to hang with like-minded DJs who were running things in the wedding world. This was just what I needed to up my game. Get me to the next level and more lucrative gigs.

The following Wednesday, I made sure I was a bit early.

I saw a long table with ten chairs around it and a RESERVED sign on it.

This must be the place, I tell myself.

I take my drink and mingle. I see Hansen walk in with some other people. Hansen nods over to me and makes the introduction.

"You must be the infamous DJ BFAD!" Seymour holds out his hand to shake and gives me an unnecessarily long and much too firm handshake. "Here nice and early. I like that. Shows initiative."

As the other DJs show up, I don't recognize any of them. They grab drinks from the bar, ignore me and sit down. I make sure to grab a spot at the end of the table for a quick getaway if needed. After some forced chit-chat and general introduction, Seymour formally starts the meeting.

"Fellas, we are the best wedding DJs in the city. So why are we getting paid less than what the florist or wedding cake designer makes?" he asks while giving each of us direct eye contact and continues. "Serious question, fellas. I think tonight we should get down to pricing and what everyone is charging. Let's up our game. If we all raise our prices, the couples will have no choice to pay what we are worth!"

I kept things close to my chest. I thought my prices were fair—my customers seemed to think so too. But the other professional wedding DJs? They were obsessing over who was charging what. If your prices were too cheap, you were "lowering the value" for the industry. If your prices were too expensive, you were "gouging the customer" and making the industry look bad. They insisted on keeping our prices competitive, but these sharks would undercut your price in a heartbeat.

It was a no-win situation.

Seymour pulled out his laptop from his bag. The next topic of conversation was where we were working and how we were getting business. He attempted to get a round table conversation going as a general topic of interest. He disguised it as making sure we all had enough venues and gigs to go around, but secretly I was convinced he was trying to see how he could undercut us.

I kept tight-lipped.

"Okay, team. We're going to go around the table. Everyone is going to say where they have an exclusive contract; that way, we won't book where our fellow members are working," Seymour says while banging away on his keyboard.

I happen to be sitting at the end of the table as he looks in my direction.

"Let's start with you, Mr. Brent."

"Ummm, I've been here and there. I'm not that busy, really," I say, trying to dodge the question.

"Well, that's not what I've been hearing, BFAD," Seymour smirks. "I heard you were at Chez Bleu last week, snazzy place; sounds like you've been a busy guy."

How does he know I was at Chez Bleu? Jacob must have told him. Was that one of Seymour's venues? I must have inadvertently stepped on his toes.

I downplay it. "Oh yeah, I had a gig there recently, I forgot."

"Forgot . . ." Seymour says, using air quotes with his fingers.

The other DJs sitting around the table were more than happy to interrupt and humble-brag about their exclusive venues.

"I've been at the Fairmont Hotel now for 15 years," another DJ with a goatee pipes in. "Nobody is taking that from me. They love me there!"

"I have exclusive contracts at The Marriott and Richmond Golf Course," another joins in. "They won't have any other DJ there; I give them a 10% kickback when I book, so I know none of you guys are going there," he looks over at me and winks.

Seymour types it all into his computer keyboard.

I couldn't wait until this brag-fest was over. It was unbearable.

For months after, Seymour continued to send over communications about future meetings. But I always declined. After a while, he stopped. I was relieved, one less hassle to worry about. I didn't think much about it until about a year later . . .

The ballroom was wall-to-wall packed. In fact, you couldn't even see the floor. There must have been around 300 people crammed into the small ballroom. I'm weaving my way through the crowd back to the DJ booth located up on the balcony.

As I maneuver my way through the crowd, I feel my left arm being grabbed.

I turn around to see Seymour!

What's he doing here? Have they booked another DJ tonight?

"What are you doing here?" he asks bluntly.

"I'm DJing up there," I point to the balcony. "I start in 10 minutes. How about you?"

"I'm performing . . ."

"Performing?" I say—a mixture of surprise and curiosity in my voice.

"Seymour the Supernatural," he says, handing me a business card, a picture of him using the hypno-hands and a mesmerizing stare on the front.

"Magician?" I ask. My face scrunches up, not quite sure if he's pulling my leg.

"Magician, Comedian, Illusionist, you name it. I'm an overall world-class entertainer!"

Wait, this was the same guy who had 20 guys out rocking weddings all over the city on any given Saturday?

"What about Seymour Sounds?" I ask.

"Listen, BFAD, let me give you some free advice. It's all about entertainment. Weddings are dead. This overall entertainment package is where the money is at. People want to be entertained, and they will pay premium dollar for it. I'm booked solid for the next year. People are throwing money at me. I'm making three times more than you tonight!"

I should have guessed, always chasing the money.

"So you are still spinning? How did you get in here wearing that?" he asks, pointing at my outfit—a button-up Ben Sherman shirt, Clarks shoes, and fitted trousers.

"What do you mean?" I ask. It took me half an hour to pick out this outfit.

"You need to wear a tie when you come here!" he says, pointing to his tie.

I didn't have the heart to interrupt him, but he was the only one in the room wearing one. It was a super busy abstract art deco necktie like something out of the Value Village 1980s pile. It was so loud I can't stop staring at it . . . hold on, why can't I stop staring at it? Was he trying to hypnotize me?

I realize I need to run up to start the music.

"Hey Seymour, I have to jet. The show is about to begin," I tell him.

"Okay, Brent . . ." his eyes widen, and he stares directly at me without blinking. "Have a good gig . . ." his voice trails off at the end of the sentence.

"Thanks," I nod.

For a magician, he did a great disappearing act. That was the last time I ever saw or heard from Seymour.

IT'S LIKE RAIN ON YOUR WEDDING DAY

Sophie wanted an outdoor wedding.

Nobody wants rain on their wedding day. Your wedding day needs to be sunny and warm and beautiful outside. The reality is we live in Vancouver, where the weather can be unpredictable at best. We have the wettest, coldest summers on record (or so it seems), so you need to have a Plan B if having an outdoor wedding, right?

Vendors in the wedding industry tend to watch the weather forecast a bit more intensely than the average person. I mean, it can't possibly have rain on the most important day of your client's life.

As I drive to the venue, a dark storm cloud follows me. I try to outrun it, but it's still there lurking above me.

Like that scene in *Butch Cassidy and the Sundance Kid*, where they are being pursued by some faceless predators, the cloud behind me is relentless. I look again in my rearview mirror. It's getting darker and darker and more and more ominous. The wind is pushing against the car, forcing me to keep both hands on the wheel to keep it straight.

By the time I arrive at the venue, the entire sky is covered. It is so dark it feels like the middle of the night, not 2:00pm. That sun we wanted today will not be making an appearance, unfortunately.

When I open the car door, the wind forces it open with a violent gust, almost ripping my arm off. It takes both hands to slam it shut.

Some of the guests have already arrived, girls in stiletto heels wobbling in the wind, hair blowing in every direction, hands holding onto their boyfriends' shoulders for support, and holding down their dresses as the wind tries to blow it up over their heads. Men's ties are at 45-degree angles, as they try to walk in a straight line while holding decorations that are blowing sideways. It's grim.

The weather gods have spoken. *Today will be an inside ceremony,* I tell myself.

I walk inside to the reception room with my first load of equipment ready to unload. The catering manager, with a blue skirt and matching suit jacket, walks over to introduce herself.

"Crazy weather out there!" I tell her.

"I know . . ." she sighs. "I feel bad for Sophie; it's been looming all day," she says.

"So, what's Plan B, ceremony inside?" I ask, getting ready to unload my gear.

"No Plan B, unfortunately," she replies, a slight roll of her eyes.

"It's going to be hammering down out there in about 10 minutes!" I laugh in disbelief.

"The bride wants an outdoor wedding," she says.

"Everyone is going to get drenched; it looks like a thunderstorm! It's not safe!"

"The bride said the wedding would be outside in the rose garden or nothing. We can provide umbrellas for some of the guests, and we have a tent set up at the back for you," she offers.

"Any chance of talking her out of it?" I ask, fingers crossed behind my back.

"I tried," she shrugs.

Sophie had been planning this wedding since she was a little girl—the beautiful outdoor rose garden with 200 of her closest family and friends by her side.

I could tell even from our first meeting; she had a vision, and it was not going to be tampered with. If she wanted an outdoor wedding, she was getting an outdoor wedding. I know it's not supposed to rain on your wedding day, but this is going to be carnage. It's time for a reality check.

You can't trust your venue.

Some couples book solely on how the venue looks in the perfect online photos or wedding magazine, not taking into account there has to be a Plan B. Last summer I had wedding on top of a ski mountain, hundreds of thousands of dollars spent for the scenic view. No expense spared. Only to be met with the thickest fog I have ever seen in my life. You literally could have been anywhere in the world. Another venue burned down to the ground two weeks before the wedding.

Today we need to be inside.

Unfortunately for her 200 guests, the bride wasn't flexible.

The rain is now coming down in buckets. Grandma is soaked, kids are soaked, and everyone is pretending to be enjoying themselves.

Sophie and Henry comfortably exchange vows under the gazebo with the officiant. They are the only three dry people in the rose garden.

My DJ tent becomes a shelter from the torrential downpour. There are 20 people crowded around me, taking any bit of dry tent real estate they can. My elbows are pinned to my side; I can barely move. A smiley older Uncle thinks it's hilarious. He is cracking jokes about us being blown away. His three chubby kids are pressed up against my equipment.

The rain is sneaking through the sides of the tent, water getting closer and closer to my gear. I'm nervous. *What a lame way this would be to die,* I think to myself. I can see the headlines in the tabloids.

"DJ Electrocuted in Bizarre Wedding Ceremony Accident!!"

At this point, nobody cares about the wedding. Nobody is listening to the vows. They are being polite and pretending to enjoy themselves. I'm trying to focus. *Okay, just the Registry Signing song and Recessional need to be played before I can pack up and get back inside a dry room!*

After what seems like hours, it's finally over.

I pack up, and the wires and cables are dripping wet. My gear is soaked. I have a towel in the car that I fetch and wipe everything down with. I ask the staff for extra rags to clean off the wet grass and dirt from the speaker cable and throw it in a pile with some other wet gear. I leave it to dry. Let's hope it still works.

My shoes and socks are wet through. I take off my socks and twist them, squeezing out all of the rainwater. I stick some paper towels from the bathroom into my shoes and slip my bare feet back in. My shirt is soaked through; I try to angle the hand dryer on it. The air from it is cold, and it's making me colder. I start to shiver.

It's July, and the room is warm, but we are all freezing from being out in the rain. The floor-to-ceiling windows are steaming up. It's muggy and damp.

It's a long dinner service. The last speech has just been made; the bride and groom thank their guests for coming. It's just past 9:00pm, and I'm about to start the dance party as soon as the cake is cut and the speeches are done.

The mass exodus begins. I wish I could join them.

Chairs are disheveled, half-empty drinks are left on tables, and there's a scrum at the coat rack area. Men grab their jackets from the back of the chairs with one hand and their kids' hands with the other. Ladies grab their shawls, purses, and umbrellas. Goodbyes are at a minimum. People just want to get into their warm cars and back to their cozy houses. The 200-strong guest list dwindles down to less than 50 in a matter of minutes.

The bride is surprisingly oblivious to the situation.

"People are leaving. Can we get the dance floor going? Maybe if you play some more Top 40, that new Usher song or something?"

Nothing will ignite the damp and dreary crowd, not even the new Usher song. Bodies are disappearing quickly.

The bride looks at me with desperation. "Do something!" she says.

"You think I can save this disaster?" I say to myself. I'm wet, cold, and miserable. Her perfect wedding day is giving me pneumonia, and there was nothing I could do to save it.

The wedding vows were now over five hours ago; at that point, the wetness gets into your bones. I was envious as I watched the guests exit en masse while I stood shivering and damp for the next two hours attempting to salvage the party. We finally pulled the plug around 11:00pm, about two hours earlier than expected; it's amazing we even lasted this long.

As I leave with my equipment loaded up on the trolley, I pass Sophie, who is sitting near the entrance.

"Hey, thanks for having me," I tell her.

"Yeah, it's too bad the dance party didn't take off," she says.

"Yeah, I think everyone was just tired . . ." I lie. I hate to lie, but sometimes we need to tell little white lies to our clients. Sometimes, we even need to tell them that they are right even though we know better.

WE NEED TECHNO

Felix had wanted a raging techno dance party for his New Year's Eve wedding. He described his vision as "like being in a Vegas nightclub," so when it strikes midnight, everyone loses their minds.

There were over 300 people coming to his wedding at the casino hotel. I ran through the playlist in my head one more time. Start off with some deep house, a few mashups, then into hard house and techno.

I had only gotten this gig on the premise I could drop a face-melting techno set.

"We need techno," he told me during the consultation.

"Will your crowd like it?" I asked.

"Don't worry, I used to DJ. My crowd goes clubbing hard every weekend," he assured me and then asks, "Can you send me some samples of your mixes?"

It was the last piece of the puzzle before signing the agreement; he had to approve.

He sent me some samples that he liked, and I filled in the blanks with some banging EDM music that I had. I still wasn't convinced I could pull off an entire wedding night of it. This wasn't a club night; this was going to be all ages and all demographics.

I spent the last few days before the gig honing my skills on the decks and downloading a batch of brand new remixes and mashups that I thought would go over well. I wanted this to be the epic dance party Felix had envisioned. I did not want to disappoint.

I show up at the venue three hours before any of the guests to set up. I want to be prepared for the rowdy crew that will be partying the night away with me.

Soon, the first guest shows up, an old dude in his 80s hunched over with a cane. Then another elderly couple arrives. Later, a middle-aged family shows up with a toddler and a newborn. The woman looks exhausted, and the husband is trying to wrangle the older of the two toddlers from climbing up on the table.

Okay, this is not the crowd I was expecting.

Guests continue to arrive—grandparents, uncles, aunts, families, kids, and babies. I double-check everything on my schedule to make sure this is the right room; I do a quick walk around to make sure I'm in the right place.

There are only two tables of friends. Maybe 30 people out of the 300 guests that I can see. And at least one of the tables looks like the contents of the Australian rugby team. Giant men squeezed into tight suit jackets. They look like they are more into Slayer and Metallica than any of the techno on my playlist.

As the party gets started after dinner, one of the older grandparents requests Michael Buble's "Sway" so they can practice their ballroom dancing.

I groan. This crowd is nothing like Felix described.

I start off with some of the more mellow beats from the playlist. The room is dying. The crowd is definitely not digging it; they are leaving in droves. People start to gather their coats, jackets, and strollers.

By 10:32pm, the place is practically deserted. Even the two tables of friends are not dancing. I could blame the groom's taste in music, but it's all my fault that I agreed to it. I'm the one who looks like an idiot. I can't take it anymore. It's gone on too long.

"You taking requests, mate?" a thick Aussie accent asks.

I look up to see what can only be described as a Human Refrigerator towering over me. He's easily one of the biggest dudes I have ever seen. The beer can in his enormous hands look like one of those miniature pop cans. His button-up white dress shirt looks ready to rip open Hulk style with the flex of a muscle.

"Anything you want, buddy," I reply instinctively and nod.

"Zac Brown Band, Chicken Fried," he says. Then turns and walks away.

Shit, a country song. It's not a bad country song, but Felix will not be happy.

For a little while longer I keep the techno going. Waiting for the right moment to mix in a country song. One song mixes into the other into the next one. It must have been too long because the Human Refrigerator is back.

"CHICKEN FRIED NEXT!"

With a trembling finger, I cut the current track playing. You could almost hear the track get ripped off halfway through. This party is a bust; I might as well go down swinging. I play his song, and a few people get up. It's an emergency, so I drop Outkast's "Hey Ya" afterwards and gather a few other stragglers to the dance floor. Please, please, please stay until at least midnight. I will play anything you want.

Keeping my head above water, I grab any of the last remaining 50 or so guests, playing whatever they want to hear. Random requests played by a desperate DJ including Frank Sinatra, Hall and Oates, Earth Wind and Fire, Top 40, and some Salsa.

At 11:59pm, I start the New Year countdown. The place looks barren.

10

9

8

7

6

5

4

3

2

1

"HAPPY NEW YEAR!" I shout a bit louder than necessary into the mic, trying to disguise the fact that the room is almost completely empty. A few lackluster whoops, a few limp high-fives; it's definitely not a night anyone will remember.

As I pack up, I can't help thinking I ruined his wedding and everyone's night. I just couldn't find that middle ground. I should have been more assertive about his techno vision and been upfront with him that it would never have worked with this crowd.

"Sorry, man," I offer Felix a half-hearted apology for not sticking to his list.

I offer my hand, but he declines to shake it. His bride grabs his shoulder and looks at me.

"You did what you had to do," she offers.

Sometimes doing what I think is right can turn out to be very wrong . . .

VOLUME CONTROL

I get a tap on my shoulder; it's the server who gave me a bread roll earlier. I pull the left earphone from my head and give her a nod, "Hey!" I shout over the music.

"You need to turn it down!" she shouts back.

I'm into the third song of my two-hour set. My speakers are only at 50%, and the mixer is nowhere near the reds. Usually, after the first song or two, the energy dips a bit while people grab another drink and go back to mingling. Not tonight. As of now, nobody has left the floor. Everyone is on the dance floor, including grandparents to the bride's teenage nephews. So far, my night is going exactly as planned.

"Too loud?" I ask.

"My manager told me to tell you that this is a residential area, and the police will show up," she says with the look of someone who would rather be anywhere else. The manager sent her in to do his dirty work, and she looked like she wanted to leave.

"Okay, no problem," I make a grand gesture of turning down the volume.

Any lower, and we'll be able to hear people talking in the background and lose the party vibe I desperately need. As she walks away, I sneak the volume back up to the original level. *Okay. That's better*, I think to myself. If it's too low and you can practically hear people talking on the dance floor, you need that sweet spot of volume that's loud enough to dance to but not too loud that it gives you a headache. As I line up the next song, the crowd makes a circle around the bride and groom. They jump around and take a minute to share a kiss.

"Whoooo!" one of the cousins shouts. The best man turns around and gives me a high-five.

This is the moment a wedding DJ lives for. Just then, I get another tap on my shoulder. This time, it's the manager.

"Right down, buddy!" he says, using his finger pointing toward the ground to emphasize every syllable. "This is a residential area; the police will come, and I don't need it."

"Okay, no problem," I tell him. He watches as I slightly turn down the volume controls. This time, turning it down about 20% on both the mixer and reaching over to twist the Yorkville's volume down, so I can't push it louder even if I wanted to.

"More!" he nods, arms crossed.

"More? They will barely hear it . . ." I plead.

"Turn the music down, or I'm shutting it down!" he stares for an extra second to make his point.

I turn it down so low I can almost hear the conversation on the other side of the room.

Heads turn in my direction.

I'm less than 30 minutes into a three-hour party. Who do you think looks like the killjoy? The venue manager? No, the DJ is deliberately sabotaging the party by turning the volume down.

This wedding venue is one of the most prestigious in the city—it's a status symbol. I'll never know why. As I pulled into the parking lot to load in today, I had to pass a gang of staff smoking at the side of the building. The tall one puts out a cigarette looks me in the eye and spits on the ground. Hard to believe this place has a two-year waiting list for a peak summer Saturday. They pack in the bookings sometimes 2-3 weddings a day. A quick one in the morning, an afternoon lunch ceremony and an evening reception. A general assembly line for weddings. It's right in the middle of a swanky million dollar neighborhood. If one of the older residents sitting in their waterfront mansion picks up the phone to call the police, this party is over. I wish I could warn couples not to book here. I always try my best to work with both the couple and the management. I don't want to burn any bridges, but tonight, I can't keep either party happy.

"What are you doing man, turn it up!"

"Sorry Derek, the manager wants it at this level . . ."

"Fuck the manager, crank it!"

"He said something about this being a residential neighborhood, and the police might get called."

"I don't give a shit; he was more than happy to take my money when we booked here! Crank that shit."

I nod at him, "I hear ya, dude."

I sheepishly push up the volume; Derek motions with his hand an upward motion.

"More! Crank it!"

I turn the volume up and down game for the next two hours—up, down, up, down, as I get some more shoulder taps and police threats. The police never arrive.

Ten minutes before lights on, I get another shoulder tap. By now, I was livid.

"Nobody is going to close down the party at 12:50am, for fuck's sake!"

The dance floor is full, and every person is still here in this room. Young or old, every song is killing it. It's an epic party, yet I had spent more time discussing my speaker volume than concentrating on the party!

It's 1:00am on the dot, and the party is finally done when I get a "ONE MORE SONG! ONE MORE SONG!" chant.

The manager has already put up the full house lights as he stands beside me, pointing at his watch. Derek, the groom, comes up to the DJ booth and gives me a massive handshake, coming in close to my ear.

"You fucking killed it tonight! Best DJ ever, how about one last song?"

I had no choice and played one last party anthem singalong cranked at absolute maximum volume.

I never played at that venue again. I got a lifetime ban, but it was worth it. Sometimes things don't work out, but then again, sometimes they do. What's for you won't go by you.

NEVER TOO LATE

David and Madilyn wanted to meet me in a coffee shop to discuss their wedding at 1:00pm on a Thursday. I had no idea about the details, guest count, or even location—I had only received an email asking to meet up to discuss their wedding. Fine by me, so far it was easy enough, if only I wasn't running late.

"Damn, I hate being late," I mumble under my breath. I'm stuck in traffic on my way to 49th Parallel on Main St. I'm only five minutes late, but still, I like to make a good first impression.

As I swing open the door to the coffee shop, I give a quick scan of the room to realize the couple is late too. There was nobody else in the coffee shop apart from an older couple in their 70s.

Lucky break, I think to myself; I can grab a coffee and relax for a minute or two before they arrive. I get my order and take a seat by the door, ready to greet the couple as they walk in. Taking a sip of my large dark roast, I look around and recheck the time.

I can see the older couple trying to make eye contact with me. They sat side-by-side holding hands at the next table. The gentleman has a warm smile with a head full of white hair.

"Wedding DJ?" he asks.

"Yes . . ." I nod my head, smiling back. *Maybe the couple's parents,* I think to myself.

“I’m David,” he gets up from his seat, holding out his hand, “nice to meet you.”

I realize it’s the couple I’m supposed to meet. I take my coffee and sit down and listen to their love story. They were high school sweethearts who moved apart during their college years. David moved to the prairies for work in the 60s. Madilyn married, had kids, and became widowed. They never saw each other for the next 45 years until David bumped into Madilyn at a friend’s dinner party by chance.

“That was last year,” she smiles at David.

“We haven’t been apart a day since,” Madilyn adds.

I’ve met hundreds of couples for a wedding consultation over coffee, and one thing I knew for sure was they were madly in love—touching each other’s hands, laughing. The 70-year-olds in front of me were about as happy and content in each other’s company as any of the couples I had met.

We chat about the wedding. They want it to be very traditional and small.

“Our grown-up kids will be there,” says David.

“And grandkids,” Madilyn adds with a laugh.

“Life’s too short,” he tells me while holding Madilyn’s hand.

The wedding, as expected, was loving, and everyone got along great. There were no politics. It was a super chill vibe.

Straight after the ceremony, the photographer gathers the entire room of guests and arranges them for a single group shot. The group includes the five or six grown kids from both sides, the friends, and the grandkids.

"Great shot!" I told him during the reception.

"Yeah, that one's a keeper!" he smiled.

The wedding was more than a paycheck, more than playing ABBA; I had an obligation to make the day as memorable as I could. Why not? I'm there anyway. Why not give that extra little bit?

Two years later, I ran into the same photographer at another wedding.

"Hey, I'm sorry I have a terrible memory," he says. "I know we worked together recently but not sure where . . ."

"From David and Madilyn's wedding," I tell him.

The penny drops. "Yes, of course!" he says, shaking my hand.

"They were so great," I add.

"Yes, they were the nicest couple . . . I'm not sure if you've heard . . ." he pauses for a second and explains that David had died a few months earlier. Apparently, Madilyn had told him the news while ordering some of the wedding photographs to be put into a memorial album.

"I'm sorry to hear," I tell him. "They were such a lovely couple."

"The funny thing is Madilyn wasn't sad when I spoke to her. She told me the wedding was the happiest day of her life."

CHAPTER 14

ANOTHER SATURDAY NIGHT

"My friend Lisa from work is having a BBQ next Saturday," Emma says between sips of coffee.

I shift uncomfortably in my chair.

"I know, I know, you're working," with an emphasis on "working," she says before I get a chance to answer.

"Yep, another fun-filled wedding," I answer sarcastically.

Another Saturday night, another wedding to look forward to. And another missed social event. Since 2009, I've missed my own friends' weddings, family outings, friends' backyard BBQs, and beach days. Friends have moved on; I no longer get invited to events.

The answer is always, "I can't, sorry working." So after a while, people stop asking. I see events that I could have been at posted all over social media. Everyone in my immediate social circle getting pinged and added.

But couples book up to a year in advance; they want to make sure they get the best vendors for their big day. It's quick money now, but a year from now, you have to honor the gigs that you booked. It's difficult to break that cycle.

At first, it was okay, I didn't mind missing an event here or there, but then every Saturday, almost every weekend of the year, is gone.

Did you ever consider having your birthday drinks on a Tuesday night? I feel like asking. Nobody is available when I'm around. You find yourself alone in no-man's land. Thursdays, Fridays, Saturdays, sometimes Sundays, then Monday to recover so you can be back in shape by Tuesday. Of course, I want to go to Lisa's BBQ; it's going to be a million times more fun than next Saturday's wedding.

Who knows, maybe this one will be different?

TURN IT DOWN

But of course, it isn't . . .

It's been a tough crowd to read, but I think I've cracked it. It's not a wild dance party, but it's good enough. It's not rocking, but it's what I expected tonight, considering it was a quieter, older crowd with kids. I mean the bride was heavily pregnant, must have been at least 7 months. There was no way she was going to party tonight. Still, I managed to get a small group up to dance by playing their throwback requests and desperately trying to keep the energy going.

The bride walks up to the DJ booth. I take off my headphones and give the biggest smile I can manage.

"Hey, how's it going!" I say enthusiastically. Out of everybody in the room tonight, her feedback is the only one that matters.

"Umm, good . . ." she replies. Her face is deadpan with no smile.

Thoughts quickly race through my head. *Is she happy? Does she think I'm doing a good job? Maybe I'm going to get a compliment, even a tip?*

"Could you turn down the music, please?"

"Down?" I repeat back. Not what I was expecting; you could barely hear the music as it was.

"Yes, down, please. It's too loud. We are trying to talk," she turns and walks away.

I discreetly turn the volume control all the way down, almost to the point of silence.

You can hear the remainder of the guests talking over the music. It's complete background noise at this point. The last dozen or so people left on the dance floor shrug their shoulders and leave. Everything just kind of fizzles out, and the night is over. I should be happy, it's getting late, and I get to pack up and get out of here, but it's a pride thing. I don't want to be that kind of DJ that nobody will remember a year from now.

No compliment, no tip. Why am I even here?

JOB INTERVIEW

"That's it! I need a real job," I confess to Emma the next morning.

"You have a job," she says.

"No, I mean a job job," I answer back.

I mean, this wedding DJ gig was fun and everything, but now it was time to get back to a regular nine-to-five professional job. I longed for a simple, easy life, punching in and out with zero stress. Regular hours, health benefits, and a predictable day. Definitely a job that didn't rely on pleasing strangers for approval.

And with that, the job hunt begins. Well, as much as a 10-year hiatus in job hunting can go. I'm mainly scrolling through my LinkedIn contacts and random Vancouver software companies to see where my friends work.

One night, I stumble upon an almost identical role that I had been fired from. By coincidence, I know someone who works there. I did him a few favors back in the day; hopefully, he hasn't forgotten. I start texting him.

Hey Brendan, I see your company is hiring!

Yeah, Brent, you looking?

Yep, the role looks similar to the one I had at XIZ.

Totally, pass me your resume, and I'll get it to the right people!

I frantically update my resume; there's a huge gap between 2009-2017. Self-employment gives you a lot of "soft" skills, but I can't exactly write down that I get along well with the photographer. Of course, Brendan has an incentive to get my resume in the hands of HR. In the software industry, a referral hire usually comes with a little reward in the form of a $2,000 bonus.

A couple of days later, an email pops up in my Inbox. It's an interview with someone named Amanda—*informal, coffee shop, next week if that works?*

We quickly organize a time and place, and I ask if there is anything I need to prepare.

Nope, I look forward to meeting up. Brendan says you were great to work with!

Bingo, I'm back in the saddle! I got this!

I have the music cranked up, and I'm in a great mood as I drive to the interview. *It's my lucky day,* I think to myself, as I find a perfect parking spot right across the street from the busy downtown coffee shop. I'm a few minutes early. JJ BEAN downtown is where I would usually meet up with a client, but today, I'm getting interviewed for a real job.

A text pops up on my phone.

Running late, there in 15 minutes.

It's a freezing wet Sunday afternoon in October, and I'm shivering outside. There were no seats inside the coffee shop where we were supposed to meet, so I've had to settle for a cold metal chair under the awning on the patio.

The devil on my shoulder urges me to reply: *Move your ass.*

The angel convinces me likewise, and I eventually text back: *All good, take your time.*

I notice a parking attendant in his bright yellow jacket across the street handing out tickets to unsuspecting parked cars and realize my meter is only good for another 45 minutes. I internally debate running down the street to pop another dollar in my meter, deciding against it as I may lose my seat. Hopefully, Amanda won't be too much longer.

This was a double referral. Not only Brendan, but another ex-colleague had put in a good word for me. I'm hoping it's a quick meeting; this will be more of a formality. A "putting-a-face-to-a-name" type of meeting. This interview is as good as sealed in my mind. I'm thinking about how I would spend my money. The nine-to-five routine and steady income would be welcome, and I'd get to switch off as soon as work was done . . . I visualize my office, desk, and the daily commute.

I grab a coffee and sit uncomfortably, laying out my leather binder on the table. "It's been a while," I laugh to myself. The girl at the table next to me gives me an awkward glance.

Amanda is late.

A girl with sandy blonde hair in her mid-20s heads straight toward me. It must be Amanda. We make eye contact, and she asks, "Are you Brent?"

"Yes, hi Amanda, good to meet you!" I hold out my hand—no return handshake.

"I'm sick," she says miserably. There's no handshake, no eye contact, and no interest.

“Oh, I’m sorry to hear,” I offer as she sits.

Papers are spilling out of her binder; she sifts through a handful of resumes until she locates mine, pulls it out, and lays it on the table between us.

“So, you worked at XIZ for a few years, good. What happened there?”

“I was um . . . laid off,” I confess. “I’ve been self-employed since 2009.”

“Right . . . okay, and what makes you want to work again for a company?”

THE MONEY

THE SECURITY

THE HEALTH BENEFITS

THE PAID HOLIDAYS

THE SOBER PEOPLE

THE NO MORE Y.M.C.A. REQUESTS

“I feel the time is right, and your company looks like something I’ve been waiting for.”

“Right, what training have you had lately in the latest CRM programs?” she dials straight in.

“Ummm . . . nothing lately, as I said, I’ve been self-employed but I . . .”

“I’m trying to see how you would benefit our company. Could you let me know any skills or benefits that would set you apart from the other candidates?”

“I’m a self-starter, I can proactively . . .” I drift off, not finishing my sentence, noticing that Amanda is completely zoned out. Nothing I say will impress her in the next few minutes. It's like a bad first date. We both realize it's not the right fit, and there's no chemistry here. I'm simply a warm body making up the numbers for her candidates. For all I know, they've already hired somebody for the role.

"Okay, good. How would your self-starting qualities benefit our company?"

"Well, I've been running my own company for the past eight years," starting my list, "I do all the marketing, all the bookings, and all the networking."

"Great . . ." she is not interested. "Tell me a little bit more about your latest software skills and maybe some recent training you've had?"

She then puts her head down and starts texting on her phone. It's obvious we're both just wasting our time.

"I'm sorry, have I missed something?" I ask.

"What do you mean?" she asks, looking up from her text.

"You have my resume in front of you," I can feel myself holding back, slight irritation growing in my voice. "You can see I haven't worked for the past eight years, I'm self-employed, no software training. Nothing since XIZ."

"Then where do you think you would fit into this company?" she asks.

I'm a total fraud; what do I have to offer?

"Nowhere, as you can see by my resume, I'm just a wedding DJ."

"Thanks for your time. I think this interview's over," Amanda says with an annoyed look. I've wasted her time; I wish my resume looked different, but it doesn't. I grab my coffee and professional-looking leather case, which I didn't even get a chance to open, angry at myself and the entire interview process.

As I push the door open, I can see the bright yellow parking ticket sticking to my driver's side window.

"Yep . . . just a fucking wedding DJ," I say to myself as I rip the ticket off the driver's side window.

CHAPTER 15

HEAD DROP

I'm standing in the middle of a futuristic street parade. It's a celebration. Caravans of space vehicles pass me by while crowds of thousands cheer.

"Daddy!" a distant voice calls.

Wait . . .

The Millennium Falcon stops in front of me, the pilot opens the cockpit door at the top, and I can see him in the distance as he motions me to come forward. Two guards dressed in futuristic military uniforms escort me through the crowd and assist me up a ladder to the cockpit.

"Daddy!" the voice calls again.

The image slowly disintegrates.

"Daddy! I'm thirsty!" blurry reality appears. It's Samuel, my 3-year-old calling from the next room. Stumbling up out of bed into darkness, I open the bedroom door and make it to the boy's shared room.

"Daddy's here. I will get you water, but please be quiet, don't wake up your brother," I whisper. Then proceed to fumble down the stairs in the dark toward the kitchen to grab a sippy cup of water.

My bare feet hit the kitchen floor. A few steps in, I feel something warm oozing between my toes.

"What the . . ." I lift my foot up, struggling to keep balance. "Georgie!" I growl as the smell hits me. Dog diarrhea, fucking great! Our beloved family dog left me a present. That half-eaten sandwich she gobbled up in the park didn't sit too well in her stomach.

Hopping on my one clean foot over to the kitchen light, I flick it on. I look at the clock on the oven. It's 3:54am; I'm now wide awake, and the Millennium Falcon is long gone.

Trying to be quiet as I wash my foot, I grab a handful of paper towels and lift my foot up to the kitchen faucet to douse my foot with water while wiping it down with paper towels. I grab another handful to mop up the rest of the smelly brown sludge Georgie had left behind. Samuel is still calling me from upstairs. I pray he doesn't wake up his brother. If both are up, we will never get back to bed, and I don't need an early start today.

I quickly throw all the paper towels into the bin, grab Samuel's water, and bolt back upstairs to find Noah, his baby brother, now starting to wake.

"Daddy, what's going on downstairs?" Samuel asks sleepily.

"It's all okay, here's your water. Go back to bed, buddy . . ."

Noah is starting to fuss. I'll get him.

I run back downstairs to grab Noah a bottle of milk and make it back upstairs as fast as I can. The two boys are now giggling. Quickly, I pass Noah his bottle of milk, lift up Samuel in one arm, and bring him to our room. He'll have to sleep here for the rest of the night, so he doesn't keep his brother awake.

"What's going on?" Emma asks in a sleepy voice.

"Georgie had diarrhea!" I whisper angrily. "I slipped in it while getting Samuel's water!"

I can hear her giggle under the covers.

"If it's so funny, you clean it up next time!" I throw on some tracksuit bottoms, shut the bedroom door, and head back downstairs. I grab the dog's leash to take her out for a walk around the block so she can empty her dodgy stomach.

When I get back into the house, I check the clock on the oven; it's 4:21am, and I'm now wide awake.

I grab a blanket and try to get settled on the couch. Eyes forced shut, I'm desperate to visit that futuristic space parade again. I never realized how uncomfortable this couch was. Tossing and turning, I get up to check the clock.

It's now 5:17am, and I start thinking about the wedding I have booked today. It's my second one this weekend. Do I have all of my music ready? I forget what the couple's first dance is. I must have it written down somewhere. Thoughts start to blur, and I feel like I've just dozed off when I hear Noah wake for the day. It's 6:41am.

Nope, there's no way I'm getting back to sleep now, I think to myself; it's going to be a loooooong day.

I'm waiting for a parking space outside the restaurant we are going to for a family lunch. It's the most direct spot that leads into the front door. It's also a busy downtown street, so parking is tight.

I wait patiently.

As I'm stopped and indicating right, the car I'm waiting for pulls out, and another one swoops beside me and takes the spot. It takes every fiber of self-control not to lay on the horn. After a few seconds, I cool down a bit and eventually see a space a few spots down. After pulling in and turning off the ignition, the driver of the other car that stole my spot gets out—a young girl in her early 20s. She looks at the DJ logo on the side of the car.

As I open the car door, she shouts, "Hey, are you DJ BFAD?"

"Yes," I reply under my breath, feeling utterly annoyed as I grab Noah's car seat out of the backseat.

"Oooomigod, I'm meeting you next week!" she shrieks. "I'm Karen! I have a consultation for you to do my wedding at Cecil Green!"

My face immediately morphs from the angriest man in the world to Mr. Rogers. "Oh, Karen, of course! How are you? So nice to meet you," I slushily answer back.

Dodged a bullet.

Emma and Samuel find a table in the restaurant while I take Noah for a walk around the block. He was unsettled, tired, and crying. I try to get him to have a nap so we can eat in peace for 30 minutes and have a nice relaxing family lunch before today's wedding.

The stroller cost a fortune. Since we had less baby stuff to buy this time, as we already had lots of hand-me-downs from Samuel, we decided to splurge and pick this up from a specialty baby emporium. It had lots of neat gadgets, including an adjustable piece in the main carriage that you could place the car seat right on top of to save waking up the baby when you left the car.

To calm him down, I decide to unstrap his car seat buckle and pick him up.

I jiggle him a bit and walk around the block; he eventually nods off. He's a quick sleeper, unlike Samuel. I gently place him back in the car seat, leaving it unbuckled so I don't have to move his arms all around and disturb him. He's not going anywhere.

It was a nice quiet lunch that went better than expected. With a sleeping baby beside me and a semi-chilled-out toddler, Emma and I ate our meals without rushing and could actually taste the food instead of shoveling it into our mouths like we usually do when trying to juggle the two kids. We even managed to have a conversation for the first time in what seemed like weeks rather than the "when did you last change his diaper?" shouting we seem to do from one room to another.

As we walk back to the car, I notice I have a big smile on my face. Life is good.

The July sun is beaming down. It's so hot that Georgie had to be leashed up outside the restaurant in the shade while we ate our lunch. She didn't mind though, some of the staff fed her some scraps and gave her a fresh bowl of water. Even the dog is having a nice day.

I think about how much pressure I put on myself. Bringing the entire family to a restaurant for lunch, including the dog, is quite the feat. I give myself an internal pat on the back. I get so envious of the neighbors—they strap on their backpacks, throw the baby in the back, and hike up Cypress Mountain like it's no big deal. Their pictures on Facebook show a smiling happy family in the mountains with the sun shining and two kids almost the same age as ours. Underneath, I see comments saying things like, *wow, you guys are amazing! What a beautiful family! Amazing moments that will last forever.*

I've posted about three family pictures on Facebook, and in all of them, I have baby spit up on my shirt and dark circles under my eyes from lack of sleep. I'm struggling to keep my head above water most of the time. The general perception is that you need to be Super Dad. The whole world is watching, all the time.

Yesterday, at the school park, when I picked Samuel up from class, he informed his classmates, at the top of his lungs, that the other night, "Daddy said the F-word!"

"Uh, hehe, no I didn't, Samuel," I try to convince him that he had misheard me.

"Yes, you did, you said *fucking*!" he shouts loudly, his friends giggling. Other parents turn their heads in my direction. I can feel my face turning red.

"You got it wrong Samuel, Daddy actually said frucking . . . frucking . . . is a type of . . . bird call . . ." I trail off, a bead of sweat forming on my brow as the other 6-year-olds stare me down.

In the 80s, I don't remember dads doing as much with their kids as we do now. They were the breadwinners, the sole providers in the family. They worked hard all week and then played golf or lazed on the couch with a beer all weekend. Now, we need to reassure ourselves and everyone around us that not only are we the providers, we are raising spiritual, loving, and open-minded individuals. It's a juggling act that we are all conforming to. No other male in the history of the planet has done more for their kids than our generation. Yet, it still never seems like enough.

To my surprise, Noah is still sleeping in his car seat while we stand at the car door. Emma and Samuel climb in and buckle up. I gently detach the car seat from the stroller and start to move it inside the car. I feel something heavy slide out.

Thump!

My son's newborn head hits the pavement. It sounds like a watermelon falling from a four-story balcony. And then comes the blood-curdling-every-parent's-worst-nightmare-infant-scream.

"What happened?" Emma asks, obviously concerned, as she grabs Noah off the ground.

His tiny face is cut up, and his forehead is swollen. He is screaming.

"Daddy, what happened to baby Noah?" Samuel asks, breaking into tears.

The scene is growing, and there are about 15 bystanders now crowding around. A voice announces that they have called 911. A lady working at the bakery beside the restaurant runs out, ushering us into her shop for shelter. We all run in.

One lady in the parking lot is freaking out on me because I've put Georgie into the car on a hot day.

"Not now, lady, please, not now!" I yell.

Emma is the only one holding it together.

How could I forget to buckle him in? The late nights and lack of sleep have turned my brain to mush.

"This is all my fault!" I scream in my head. "I'm so tired from all these fucking weddings!"

We have spent so much time creating, nurturing, and loving this little helpless human, and I didn't buckle in the car seat! How could I be so stupid?

Sirens wail as the ambulance arrives.

My pocket vibrates, I instinctively check my phone.

Google Calendar Reminder: Mike and Tina's wedding in three hours.

HAPPY

Mike and Tina's wedding was very low on my list of places I wanted to be today. I constantly check my phone for updates on Noah. He's fine. Emma even sent a picture of him laughing when the doctor checked on him, but I'm still a nervous wreck replaying the afternoon's events in my mind.

When I met Mike, the groom, and Tina, the bride, I knew there was only one song for their first dance.

"Proud Mary" by Ike and Tina Turner.

I mean, what other choice was there? How could it be any other way?

When I mentioned it over our coffee meeting, it was met with two straight faces. No expression, nothing.

"Proud Mary," I said again, this time emphasizing the names, "you know by IKE and Tina Turner? Mike and Tina? IKE and Tina?"

They had never heard of it; they didn't even crack a smile.

I sing a line in vain.

♫ *Rolling! Rolling! Rolling on the river!*

My age gets the best of me sometimes, and I let it drop.

"We are going for a roaring 20's theme with an electro swing music vibe" he tells me deadpan "we are then going to transition into "Happy" by Pharrell as the main song of the night".

I sigh.

"Happy" by Pharrell Williams. It's up there with the Y.M.C.A. for cheese factor as far as I am concerned. But as cheesy as it was, it became the wedding anthem that summer.

Everyone was "Happy." Couples were "Happy." "Happy" was the song everyone wanted to hear. By the end of the summer of 2014, everyone, including me, was sick of it. It was all over the radio and internet, and featured in every meme and viral dance.

But here we were, years later, and Mike and Tina insisted. "Happy" summed up their relationship and their big "happy" day. I let out an internal groan. It was to be played at least three times: for their Grand Entrance, First Dance, and Grand Exit. I tried to explain playing any song three times in a night is "a bit" over the top, but they were not having it.

They had contacted me through my favorite wedding planner, Misha.

"We originally got in touch with PERFECTLY PRINCESS WEDDINGS, but they didn't have the day available, so they referred us to Misha," Mike told me.

I knew by now, PERFECTLY PRINCESS WEDDINGS attracted high-maintenance clients. Some planners just seem to attract pretentious couples, but if this was coming via Misha, I could get on board. We always had fun working together.

Mike and Tina arrive 25 minutes after our scheduled time with no apology. Then they spend upward of 10 minutes deciding what drink to get, changing their minds constantly.

Within minutes of sitting, Mike grabs his buzzing phone, "Hold on, I have to take this," he says while jumping up from the table and leaving me hanging mid-sentence.

A few minutes later, Tina's phone is ringing an irritatingly loud bird chirping noise from her purse. She digs around and pulls it out. "This is important," she says to me as she gets up from the table. I can hear her talking a few feet away. "Oh nothing . . . no, just a meeting our wedding planner recommended . . ."

I was quickly losing my patience. This is taking twice as long as it should. Once back at the table, they continued asking the stereotypical questions couples are supposed to ask a DJ before they hire them.

- Do you bring lights?
- Do you require a meal?
- Do you have previous reviews we could see?
- Do you take requests?

I answer a quick "Yes," to every single question, hoping to roll things along.

It should have been locked in by now, I tell myself. Considering this was a Misha referral and all of this information is on my website, this all seemed redundant.

Every now and then, they look at each other and start to snicker.

"All good?" I ask as they continue giggling at their inside joke. It's not endearing.

"Oh, it's nothing," they say as they touch each other's legs under the table. I sit awkwardly staring at the ceiling, waiting until they finish.

Finally, they ask me about my price. I had already sent a quote via email, so they were obviously feeling me out for a discount. I was too expensive.

Apparently, they had a friend who could do it for half the price I was charging, and would I consider lowering my rate? I so badly wanted to politely tell them to fuck themselves, but hey, a paycheck is a paycheck, so I politely tell them my rates are fair for a professional wedding DJ.

They tell me they have a few more DJs they are going to meet before they decide.

What a complete waste of time, I think to myself and mark it down as a no-go as I walk out of the coffee shop.

About a month had gone by, and out of the blue, I received an email saying they wanted to go ahead. I couldn't believe it. There was no way I was their first choice. More than likely, the other DJs could smell a high-maintenance couple a mile away, and I just happened to be the last DJ standing. Now the question was, do I take it?

I had a gap in my calendar that needed to be filled, and well, a gig is a gig, right? I hesitantly decided to take it.

SMOKE AND MIRRORS

Social media erupts a few days before Mike and Tina's wedding. The other vendors add engagement pictures of the couple all over their Instagram accounts with the hashtag #MikeandTinasweddingday.

- **Wedding Photographer:** Picture of Mike and Tina's engagement shoot. They are standing on a beach looking lovingly into each other's eyes. *This weekend can't come soon enough when I get to see this beautiful couple tie the knot.* #MikeandTinasweddingday
- **Videographer:** Outtake from Photographer's engagement shoot, Mike and Tina walking away from the camera, down the beach. *I can't wait to see this bride and groom get married!* #MikeandTinasweddingday
- **Wedding Planner:** Same picture from Photographer's page. Mike and Tina, beach, lovingly, eyes. *Only two more sleeps until Mike and Tina become husband and wife! Eeeeek! I am so excited for this couple's wedding. I can't wait!* #MikeandTinasweddingday #cantwait #soexcited #mrandmrs #weddingofthecentury #truelove #weddingmagic #lovemyjob #lifeofaweddingplanner #ihavethebestcouples #seeyouSaturday

At the end of the day most of us are in it for the money. It seems a little disingenuous to be so overly enthusiastic.

After the wedding, all the vendors get back onto social media to tag each other and talk about how amazing Mike and Tina's totally average wedding was. It's all so predictable. At best, their wedding day will be a six out of 10.

Sometimes, it's legit, and you get a super amazing couple. But with Mike and Tina, it's not it. It's all smoke and mirrors . . .

Finally, the day arrives.

I show up early at the Four Seasons Hotel. From previous experience, I know the load-in is hell.

It's like the scene in the Scorsese movie *Goodfellas,* where Henry Hill is walking Karen through the back entrance of the Copacabana, as I weave and dodge chefs and waiters to navigate down a tight hallway not meant for large DJ equipment.

When I roll into the freight elevator, my shoes stick to the floor. Then, when it opens on the Boardroom or Meeting level, you are met with a maze of doorways, a flurry of staff, and more sticky floors. Then past security, the cleaning staff chatting away with bins of folded laundry, down hallways, and past kitchens. Often, even straight through the kitchen. Did you know that five-star hotel restaurants often have wedding DJs mere inches from your freshly cooked fish dinner? Finally, I wheel my DJ gear from the loading bay that's covered in food slime, flies, rat traps, ooze, and grit. It's a smell that I could only assume what a dead body smells like. Most of the old hotels in Vancouver are not meant for quick in-and-out load-ins.

By the time I get to my DJ booth, I'm sweaty and filthy and ready to call it a day before I had even played a single song.

I see some of my vendor friends from previous weddings, and as expected, I discover all the vendors can't stand the couple. We start comparing notes. The videographer and photographers confirm that the couple had asked everyone for a discount using the "friend could do it half-price" trick and then piled on twice as much work as discussed.

The Photobooth Guy comes up to ask for a roll of tape to tape down some wires. He starts yapping my ear off about being a realtor and that the Photobooth thing is a part-time weekend gig. His props are haphazardly thrown together in a box: a pink boa, an Iron Man mask, Hulk fists, oversized red glasses, and a fake gold chain.

"Here, take one of my cards. If you ever need a realtor, let me know. I'll be in touch," he says as he aggressively shoves a card into my hand.

The couple is about to make their Grand Entrance. I line up "Happy" as they enter the room.

The speeches were delayed.

We were supposed to start at 8:00pm, according to the color-coded timeline. I check my phone, and it's now 8:57pm. So far tonight, Misha's schedule is airtight down to the minute. The cocktail reception, the dinner, and now the last item on the timeline are the speeches.

Misha steps up behind the DJ booth. Leaning in, she informs me with a whisper that Tina has diarrhea and has been locked in the toilet for the past half an hour. My first instinct is to laugh.

We give each a sly smile, and she fills me in. “Be ready; speeches are going to start as soon as she gets back to the head table.”

We wait.

Photobooth Guy is wandering over toward me, looking confused.

“Hey, I need you to get on the mic. I need you to announce that I lost my car keys!”

“Dude, no way! The speeches are about to start.” I tell him, reminding myself never to hire this guy as my realtor.

I play a few more background dinner songs. Still no bride. I check my phone. It’s now 9:21pm.

“Come on, Tina, let’s go!” I tell myself.

I feel a tap on my shoulder, snap off my headphones, and look to the side.

A 70-year-old uncle with a bad hair-dye job and a loud Hawaiian shirt is at the DJ booth. “I hope you fix the sound. It sounded terrible during dinner, too much bottom end.”

“Okay . . .”

Another Uncle Ray. There is always the one who knows more about the sound than me.

“You need to adjust your bass. Your mix is way off. What are you using?” he asks.

“Sorry?” I ask, unsure of the question.

"I used to be a DJ; I've done thousands of weddings."

If someone interrupts a DJ to tell them they are also a DJ, that is the sure-fire signal that they are not a DJ. A real DJ actually keeps low-key in the shadows and takes notes. *What are they playing? How is the mix? Is the crowd into it?* They're definitely not striking up a conversation while the DJ is working.

I often wonder if this ever happens to other professions. "Great service tonight, I'm also a waiter," or "Great adding up that bill, I'm also an accountant."

We are interrupted as Misha approaches the DJ booth with a change in the itinerary, looking as if she had been crying.

"Are you okay?"

"Yes, I'm fine," she says, wiping away a tear.

I know Misha better than this. "What's up?"

"Tina just said something to me. It's nothing," she replies, taking a deep exhale. "She's not happy about the wedding cake, that's all." This was also the only time I've seen a bride reduce a wedding planner to tears.

I hated this couple even more now.

After a nerve-wracking dinner, first dance, and bouquet toss, we were ready for the big party. I knew their choices would tank. They didn't want any Top 40, Hip Hop, Latin, or Classic Rock. Ugh, okay here we go . . .

I line up their Special Must Play song request list. Nothing . . .

It's bomb after bomb. A huge ballroom of 250 guests is still sitting at their tables. The dance floor is completely empty. I'm one deflated DJ.

9:34pm

Tina's bridesmaid stands in front of me, arms folded. "Mike and Tina interviewed a bunch of DJs and said you were the best."

"Well, I don't know about that . . ."

"That's what she said. DJ BFAD is the best. Prove it!" she demands.

No pressure. Sweat builds up on my neck as the dance floor sits empty. I throw everything I have at the crowd, but it doesn't budge. This gig is a dud. Soon, Misha is at the DJ booth, a sly smile on her face.

"You're going to LOVE this!" she says.

"We're being evacuated for a lame dance party?" I answer sarcastically.

"Better! The HAPPY couple is leaving!"

"WHAT? Please, tell me this isn't a joke," I can barely believe my ears.

"She's sick, stomach bug. She's been throwing up in the bathroom for the past 30 minutes, and they're heading off. She's just getting her things together."

More glorious words had never been spoken! We do a little happy dance behind the DJ booth and give a discreet high-five.

"What about the party?" I ask.

"I imagine most people will be leaving shortly after the bride and groom leave, so do whatever you want."

DJ's choice. I was on the books until midnight. Let's have some fun. All those terrible songs I had to download and prepare for their wedding?

DELETE.

A random guest comes up to the DJ booth, “Hey man, are you taking requests?”

“Sure thing” I nod my head. Thankful to be so close to the end. I’ll play anything to make the time pass more quickly.

A small crowd gathers in front of the DJ booth. I play some Top 40, Nicki Minaj, Lady Gaga, Calvin Harris, throw in some Hip Hop, and some other random requests. The next thing I know, a dance party has started.

It took forever for Tina to get her things together. I knew as soon as the bride and groom left, the party would wind down, and I could wrap things up.

Misha is back behind the DJ booth.

“When the couple leaves, you need to play their last song of the night that they wanted.”

“Happy?” I groan.

“Yes, they want to do an exit dance or something.”

Yeah, this wedding exudes happiness.

“Okay, everybody!” I start into the microphone. “Congrats to the bride and groom!”

Cheers from the crowd. “Whooooo, fuck ya!” one of the groomsmen yells. “Happy” blasts for the third time tonight through the speakers.

BOOM-BOOM-BOOM-BOOM

Pharrell rips into it.

"NOOOOOOOOOOOOOOOOOO," the once-loyal crowd is now furious.

A swarm of bridesmaids surrounds me, "Get this off, get this off! This song sucks." I sidestep around the corner, leaving my gear empty, and the song to play out to throngs of "Boooooooos!"

For this reason, I don't usually like to take a Last Song of The Night request from couples, but they insisted.

This party was definitely not ending on a "happy" note. Tina is in front of the DJ booth having a meltdown. "What are you doing?" she screams.

"It's your last song! It's on the sheet!" I tell her, picking up her itemized itinerary. I should have known better.

"Nobody likes it!" she screams.

"I can see that," I say, defending myself.

"Then change it!" she spins around, throwing up her arms. She must have realized what I tried to tell her all along—this song has a short shelf life.

The bridesmaid standing behind her shakes her head and stares me down. It's a shitty song, a shitty crowd, and a lame ending to a lame wedding. I guess I didn't prove I was the best after all.

I let the song play out; it goes on forever. The couple has left, and I breathe a sigh of relief. A weight has been lifted off my shoulders, and I feel completely relaxed. With nothing else lined up, I put on some songs I like just to fill the dead space. I'll hang back with some background music. The 250-person wedding whittles down to under 100 random hangers-on.

"Could you play something from the Space Jam movie?" The "Space Jam Theme Song" by Quad City DJ is random, but I quickly download it on the fly and drop it. Why not?

There are still about 100 people in the room. The silliness of the song lures most of the 30-somethings onto the dance floor.

The next thing I know, a party is starting, without the bride or groom! The friends gather into a circle, and people take turns strutting into the middle, showing off goofy dance moves.

I sneak a quick look at my phone. It's 10:32pm, and I have a new photo of Noah eating ice cream and laughing; he's fine.

A young girl in a red dress grabs an older white-haired uncle sitting down and pulls him into the circle. He starts to do a robot dance. Everyone looks like they are laughing or *actually* being happy?

It goes on for the next few songs; they're having a blast. And for the first time that day, I realize I am too.

LAST CALL

CHAPTER 16

DJ POO

I'm standing at the front of Samuel's second-grade class. I've volunteered as a parent for career day at his school. I have nothing prepared, so I have to think fast as twenty 8-year-olds sit on the floor staring up at me. Maybe I can ask them what their DJ name would be. This will take up a few minutes of my talk. My heart beats faster—public speaking, no matter the audience, is always difficult.

"Okay, class, I want you to think about your DJ name!" I ask enthusiastically. "Does anybody have one they would like to share?"

Hands immediately shoot into the air. "Me, me, me!" the kids cry in unison.

"Okay, you," I point to an innocent-looking girl in the front row.

"DJ POO!!" she yells; the kids howl with laughter.

"Umm . . . okay, maybe think of another name . . . how about you?" I point to a boy in the back row.

"DJ BOOBIES!!"

A hundred drunk adults and twenty 8-year-olds are not as different as you might think. After school, I ask Samuel how the kids liked my presentation.

"It was okay," he replies. "Jaden's dad is a fireman, he brought stickers."

BE CAREFUL WHAT YOU WISH FOR

People want three things at weddings: good food, free alcohol, and a great party. That's what they remember. As far as the embroidered napkins go, I guarantee they won't ever remember them. But they will always remember the party.

It's no fun when you are hired to be the life of the party, and you hate your job. When you have low vibrations and are in a bad state of mind, it doesn't take much to make you slip down a little bit further.

July 2018

I'm standing in line at Starbucks, zoned out thinking about today's wedding.

"Ommmmmmigod . . . Brent!" a voice shrieks from beside me. As I turn around, I see a woman grab her latte from the counter. Upon closer look, I realize it's Jessica.

I know more about her via my Facebook feed than any personal interaction over the past few years. I feel like I've been eavesdropping on her relationships (new boyfriend), holidays (Italy, Hawaii, France), new apartment (downtown condo), and new dog (a pug named Glitter). We worked with each other for three years at XIZ. She had survived the mass exodus, unlike me. After I left, we always meant to "keep in touch" and "meet up for a coffee," but life got in the way. Seven years later and she had moved her way up the ranks with her own corner office and trips around the world in a newly-created role I had never heard of.

"How are you!" I ask.

"Off to Vegas for a work conference in a few hours—just catching up on some work," holding up her phone.

"So you're still at XIZ?"

"Yep, heading a brand new department," she tells me, "twenty staff, we're rolling out of the new XIZ data-protection software for the North American market."

I used to know all of the corporate work lingo; now it seemed foreign to me. My new "DJ lingo" didn't translate so well to anyone outside my DJ circle. We chat for few more minutes and make a point to "connect" after she gets back from Vegas.

I noticed her shoes, Prada bag, work outfit, and expensive laptop carrier bag. *She must be making six figures,* I think to myself. I can't help wondering if I wasn't laid off, how things might have been different. Maybe I would have been the one heading a team of 20 and heading down to Vegas for a conference? I can't help feeling a little black cloud of disappointment as I grab my coffee from the counter.

"Hey Brent," she turns around and shouts back as she pulls the door open. "I'm getting married next year . . . I'll give you a call."

WHO STOLE MY SHOES?

She's wearing a red cocktail dress . . . and bare feet.

"My fucking shoes!" she shouts and pounds the table with her fist. Then she drops her head into her hands and starts sobbing.

I'm packing up my equipment as fast as possible, trying to get out of the room before this gets any worse.

"Seven! Hundred! Dollars!" She yells, startling the clean-up staff, who glide between tables collecting overturned wine glasses and broken plates, remnants of the evening's debauchery. As the cleaner pushes past her with a mop, she wails, "I knew I should have kept them on!"

Another woman in a blue ball gown approaches her and places a hand on her shoulder. "Honey," she says in a soothing voice, "I'm sure they are around here somewhere."

"Okay, okay," Red Cocktail Dress lady sobs. "You're right, you're right." Her friend continues consoling her.

"Let's just look over by the coat rack."

Her fist slams the table again. "But seriously!" she yells. "Someone stole my fucking shoes!"

The beginning of the night was sort of fun. Or at least funny. There were the usual sloppy group hugs, buddies backslapping each other, and shouting about shots. The obligatory drunk conga line formed around 10:15pm—a bit early, I thought, but still within the bell curve. One guy tried to get the group to lift him up for crowd surfing, but it flopped, and I laughed to myself. A guy with his shirt unbuttoned to his navel approaches the DJ booth.

"Heyyy, man!" he shouts, slurring even the simplest of greetings. I move closer to listen.

"Play 'Sweet Caroline,'" he asks for the tenth time. "It's my song; you need to play it next!"

One woman leans over and tries to twerk against a guy but tears her dress up the back. She doesn't notice, and neither does the guy, who is busy trying to pull his shirt over his head, snagging his face on the buttons. Another shirtless guy grabs a shiny yellow jacket and tries to put it on. He wrestles with the too-small jacket, one arm flailing around while the other remained stuck inside, before giving up and tossing it aside. It's one of those nights . . .

I've always used it as more of an end-of-the-night song to wrap up the party, but screw it! I decide to play it, get it over with, and be done with it.

It was obviously his big moment. He attempted to round up the far-too-intoxicated troops for a group singalong. I'm sure he did this at every wedding—his one party trick.

When the crowd didn't respond the way he liked, he was back at the DJ booth, yapping that I didn't hype up the crowd enough.

Whatever, buddy, I thought to myself, rolling my eyes. I had enough on my plate to worry about. I check my phone: 11:32pm. There is no way this group can keep up his pace until 1:00am. I spot the banquet manager at the back of the room, also surveying the chaos. I wave to him, and he walks over a bit earlier than usual, but we need to make the Last Call announcement.

I lean in close, "Hey Zach," I say, his name displayed on his banquet jacket name tag. "We need to call it," I tell him as I cue up the Dirty Dancing song "I've Had the Time of My Life" by Bill Medley and Jennifer Warnes.

"Technically, they have this room until 1:00am," he informs me.

We both turn just in time to see a bridesmaid running toward a groomsman standing with his arms wide open. It's the textbook final dance scene from Dirty Dancing . . . except she misses the mark and flies past the groomsman, crashing into the dance floor into a line of glasses, covering herself in a puddle of rum and cokes—the crowd cheers.

Zach purses his lips and nods.

"Call it!" he says.

I waste no time grabbing the mic, "Ladies and Gentlemen, it's the last call at the bar!"

The dance floor empties as the herd runs for refills. As they fill the dance floor once again, I sigh. By now, they are double-fisting as much as they can hold. It's now 12:02am. I take a deep breath and get back on the mic. "Thank you, everyone, for sticking around," I say, relief in my voice. "Good night, and get home safe!"

The crowd groans. I put down the headphones and start unplugging my mixer. Then the chanting begins: "One more song! One more song!"

I shoot the catering manager a look, then gesture up to the ceiling. Hit the lights!

Brightness fills the room. The once well-dressed wedding guests are now a tangled mess of bloodshot eyes, ruffled hair, and alcohol-stained clothes. Slowly, they leave the dance floor and start moving toward the exits.

Unbelievably, at the end of the night, Sweet Caroline Guy was back at the DJ booth asking for a business card. He tells me he is getting married and needed a DJ. I figured what the hell and pass him a card. He takes it and leaves. I knew I would never hear from him again.

"There is no way that this guy is going to call me," I say to myself as I reluctantly gave him a card.

As I roll out the last of my packed equipment, I can hear the girl with the red cocktail dress.

"Why?" She wails again. "Why would anyone steal my shoes!"

ALISTAIR'S WEDDING

A few months later, an email pops up in my Inbox, and to my utter disbelief, it was from Sweet Caroline Guy. Despite not hyping up the crowd enough, he wants me for his wedding. Of course, it was never going to be an easy gig. I should have known better . . .

He owned a large accounting firm downtown. The company office had a great rooftop patio with a breathtaking ocean view facing the North Vancouver mountains. It was like a living postcard, and this was today's wedding venue. For a corporate company office, it was one of the best views I've ever seen; for a wedding, it was going to be tricky. Things like running water, shelter from the elements, and protection from birds and bugs are assumed for a wedding venue. But this was a free venue, after all. I suppose it was worth the gamble.

The rooftop patio was on the twelfth floor, with metal picnic tables, concrete walls, fire sprinklers, and no outlets. There were two elevators to get up, but one was out of order. That meant there was only one elevator to get my equipment up, as well as the caterers, catering equipment, photographers, planners, and over 150 guests. The load-in was going to be fun.

I walk through an office of cubicles to get to the concrete outdoor patio for the ceremony. By the time I get everything to the rooftop, I realize it's not equipped with enough power to sustain a full-functioning wedding.

There are two outlets on the other side of the roof. I need to daisy-chain every spare extension cord and wire everything together to make it to my DJ booth. But as soon as I plug in . . .

POP!

A fuse blows, and the entire rooftop power is out. The catering staff glares at me. "Typical," I mumble and let Cassie, the wedding planner, know.

Half an hour later, the power is back on, giving me 20 minutes until guests arrive for the ceremony. I make a quick run to the bathroom to wash my hands and get ready. The office bathroom door is locked with a sign:

OUT OF ORDER, PLEASE USE WASHROOMS ON FIRST FLOOR

The bathrooms are under construction. They want us to take the elevator back down to the first floor? There's only one elevator for 150 people plus all of the vendors!

By the end of the night, the one elevator had an eye-watering stench of urine. The drunken guests obviously didn't make the two-minute trip on time, and the floor is soaked.

At least it's a cash gig tonight, I thought to myself, as Cassie hands me an envelope. I open it up and count the bills. Wait, a mistake. This can't be right. The envelope is $200 short. I recount again, "Yep, he stiffed me," I sigh. I had given him a killer deal too. We both roll our eyes when I mention it to Cassie. He bartered to get a lower price and then shortchanged me. I was kind of surprised, but at the same time, not really.

"It's short $200, and I've already given him a killer deal for a prime summer Saturday!" I tell her.

About 30 minutes later, Cassie approaches the DJ booth.

"Soooo, I've checked with the groom . . ." she starts, the tone in her voice signals I may not like what's coming next. "He said the correct amount is in the envelope; he double-checked it."

Ugh . . .

She knows, I know. It sounds like he did the rounds bartering with all the vendors. She'll mention it to him and get back to me, she says.

Thirty minutes before the ceremony, Alistair approaches the DJ booth, "Oh hey, man," he says, not looking too happy to be there. "You got the money, right? I recounted it before I gave it to Cassie. It's all there."

"It's $200 short," I tell him.

"Not possible!" he replies.

"Sorry, man, I recounted it three times myself," I say.

"We can talk about this later! I have kind of a big day ahead; I have to get ready for my wedding." He rolls his eyes, turns, and stomps off.

Now what?

For an accountant, he wasn't very accurate at counting. He was also very specific about his music, mainly wanting hardcore Hip Hop and, of course, "Sweet Caroline," which *had* to be played at his exact moment so he could do his singalong routine again. It was very important to only be played at peak time, and he would give me the signal.

With an accountant's eye to cut expenses, I wasn't provided with a tent to protect me from the blazing hot sun. My equipment is practically melting in the 35-degree heat, and after a few hours, I start to feel lightheaded and sunburnt. I make sure to grab an extra couple of water bottles, so I don't get sunstroke, only to be informed by the caterer that they had run out.

"It's so hot, everyone is drinking twice as much water as we expected," he informs me. No bother, by the time the sun goes down an hour later, the rooftop gets windy and cold, and it's time for a coffee.

Alistair struts up to the DJ booth before the speeches.

"After my speech, I'm going to drop this!" Alistair informs me while holding my $300 wireless mic.

"Please don't," I ask nicely.

He's been strutting around the patio, acting like a rockstar for the past hour. It's his BIG day, and he is going to mic drop at the end of his speech to prove how hilarious he is. Dropping a microphone intentionally after a great performance means you cannot be topped. It's intentionally damaging someone else's property; it goes beyond the value of a replacement. Whether it's your special big wedding day or not, don't even go there. Not to mention my microphone is expensive to replace.

"I have to mic drop," he says matter-of-factly. "It's going to be sooooo worth it."

I hate this guy.

"I would rather you didn't," I ask again. "It's in my contract; the client is responsible for any damages to . . ." I continue.

His focus then transfers to the bridesmaid walking past us. He loses interest in what I'm saying as he stares her up and down.

"Sorry, man," he interrupts, "it's going to make the night!" with that, he turns away and walks up to the podium.

What do I do? Options race through my mind. The best I can think of is to quickly run up to catch the mic when he's done. Instead, I wait nervously as he makes his speech. Luckily for me, all of his jokes are bombing. He is nowhere near as charismatic as he thinks he is and is getting zero laughs. He decides not to drop the mic after all.

After the speeches, we are straight into the dancing. As soon as I drop the first song, shirts start getting ripped off. Another tradition with this crew? Who knows? The groomsmen and best man start ripping off their shirts and waving them over their heads.

Okay, it's going to be one of those nights, I tell myself. I totally expected this. Luckily, I only have to spin for another hour. It's already after 11:00pm, and the music needs to be off by midnight.

Once the shirts come off, things start to get out of hand quickly. Drinks start to get thrown off the roof, and residential high-rise apartments surrounding the office start to turn on their lights. Once the drinks start flying off the roof, more and more neighborhood lights begin to turn on. What if one hits a passerby on street level? Our fun little wedding party is now turning into a legal issue. It's an accidental assault claim waiting to happen.

Not only that, the venue is a sound trap. The louder I turn up the volume to try and drown out the ruckus, the more echo bouncing off the apartments there is. This is a quiet part of town, so this is not going unnoticed. More drinks are getting thrown and smashed onto the concrete below.

The request list is out. The father-of-the-bride is not dancing. He looks at the request list, picks up the pen, and starts to scribble down a song. He is writing for what seems like a very long time. I'm curious and a little nervous. As soon as he finishes, I snatch the list and see what he's written.

Meat Loaf's "Paradise by The Dashboard Light."

"Oh geeeez," I sigh; how can I possibly play this tonight? An eight-minute 70s rock opus.

The young girls in the sparkly dresses will not be impressed. They have been telling me I've been playing old-people music for the past 20 minutes and they are songs from only five years ago. Alistair will also likely be on my case. If I drop "Paradise by The Dashboard Light," that's it; I'm done in their eyes.

However, the father-of-the-bride is important. About as important a guest as you are going to get. But so is an eight-minute empty dance floor. I have to think fast.

Then from the corner of my eye, one of the groomsmen drops his pants for no reason. Normally, I would find this unbelievable, but I can't say I'm surprised by this crowd tonight. His girlfriend is yelling at him, and I start to laugh to myself. I notice my bladder squeezing tighter, and the slightest bit of pee dribbles out.

Whoa, wait, I haven't been to the bathroom since I got here!

I notice the three empty coffee cups, two empty water glasses, an empty can of pop, and an empty beer bottle sitting on the ledge beside me.

They're all mine! Realizing my bladder is completely full, and the bathroom is on a different floor, the decision has already been made. Meat Loaf it is—my perfect Bathroom Buster Song. I will need every single second of those eight minutes.

But first, a plan.

"This one is for father-of-the-bride, Ted!"

Everyone cheers. "Let's hear it for Ted!" The twangy cheesy guitar intro to the Meat Loaf song begins. I have exactly eight minutes.

The girls in the sparkly dresses look at me like I am 100 years old. I might as well have been. They are shaking their heads, not impressed.

I run up to the group.

"I'm really sorry. I had to put this on for Ted. He's leaving soon. I won't play any more of his music. This song goes on forever; go write down whatever you want on the request list, and I promise I will play it when I get back. You have my word."

Hoping to kill two birds with one stone, Ted has his Meat Loaf and the Sparkly Dress Girls will do my work for me and fill the request list. Most importantly, I have a much-needed Bathroom Buster Song!

I run through the office toward the elevator, and hit the button what seems like 50 times, all the while feeling like I'm going to burst. I hop around, waiting for the door to open up. It seems like forever, but it finally shows up. I make it to the urinal, unzip, and Niagara Falls erupts. It keeps going and going and going, and I'm starting to think maybe eight minutes isn't long enough. I can hear the echoes of the third minute of "Paradise" echoing around the bathroom from upstairs.

Finally, the last drips are out. I zip up my fly, jump to the sink, quickly wash and dry my hands, and run back to the elevator, pressing the button another 50 times.

Finally, it opens. I jump back in and hit the button for the twelfth floor.

When it opens, I fly back through the office toward the DJ booth. I see the bride. "My dad loves this song, thank you!" she says as I run past.

"You're welcome!" I yell back.

The Sparkly Dress Girls are still there, to my surprise, huddled around the request list. I take a peek: Drake, Lil Wayne, Nicki Minaj. No problem, coming right up.

The last seconds of Meat Loaf's dramatic epic rock ballad fade out . . .

♫ *It never felt so good*

♫ *It never felt so right*

"Paradise By The Dashboard Light" was my Get Out Of Jail Free card. No more requests for Ted, I'm afraid.

From here on in, I need to please the Sparkly Dress Brigade. The Girl in The Red Sparkly Dress screams at my face as I play her first Drake request.

"Turn it up! It's not loud enough!" I oblige with a smile. One song later, she's back.

"More Drake!"

"I just played Drake; it was the last song!" I explain, but it falls on drunken deaf ears.

"I don't care!" she screams in my face.

I relent, playing more Drake and anything else they want to hear for the next hour. Justin Bieber, Tiesto, David Guetta, just cheesy club tracks to keep them at bay. No matter, The Girl in The Red Sparkly Dress wants to hear the first Drake song I played again. Not a different song, the same song—this time louder.

There are only 10 minutes to go before I can finish. Ten long minutes before I can end this nightmare of a gig.

I play her Drake song out of sheer frustration; it gets a lukewarm reception. I can't end my night like this. I cut it halfway through and drop some Snoop "Drop It Like It's Hot," and the crowd loves it. That's it! I'm done!

"Thanks, everyone, this is my last song!" I shout into the mic.

The Girl in The Red Sparkly Dress immediately runs over to complain. Fuck it. The show's over, folks. I deliberately turn the volume right down while she is in mid-scream and pick up the mic while staring into her eyes.

"Congrats to the bride and groom, and have a great night, everyone!"

She storms over to her friends on the other side of the room and points at me, scowling.

Another gong show. I'm finished at midnight. It's 11:56pm. I usually don't worry too much about the end time, but tonight I'm on the clock and punching outright at the stroke of midnight.

Alistair is suddenly standing beside me, "You need to stay!" he yells at me.

“Sorry, Alistair, I would love to, but it’s midnight.”

“No man, you have to! You didn’t play long enough because we didn’t start the party until later!”

“I can’t, Alistair, I have to close up now. It’s part of our contract, remember? Also, it’s getting late. We don’t want any noise complaints.”

While I’m tearing down, the party is still going full throttle. One of the groomsmen takes over with his own personal DJ controller and speaker that must have been stashed under one of the desks in the office. He goes straight into some techno acid fury, complete with FWAM FWAAM FWAAAM noise sound effects. He plays with no irony whatsoever and not the vibe I had left the crowd with. He’s not reading the crowd, but I don’t care. I’m out of here.

The Girl in The Red Sparkly Dress stands exactly where I need to wheel my equipment past. She makes a point to stand in my way, so I need to walk around her, shouting something as I roll my gear past her. When I turn around to hear what she has said, she stands there, giving me the middle finger. Charming, thanks for the feedback. What seems like forever, I finally get all my equipment loaded into the urine-soaked elevator and down out on the street below.

The crowd noise from the street level above is deafening. I’m actually impressed at how loud it is as it echoes down the otherwise quiet residential street. I step over the broken glass from the bottles thrown off the patio roof 12 stories up. Two police squad cars and a paddy wagon are waiting on the street. Three officers are looking upward, trying to figure which building the noise is coming from.

As I’m loading up my equipment into the back of the RAV, one of the officers gets my attention.

"Do you know where this party is at?" he asks.

"Yes, officer, right up there," I say, pointing to the roof above us.

"Twelfth floor, take the second elevator up . . ."

CHAPTER 17

PATRICK'S WEDDING

I had a bad feeling about this.

It feels like one of those heist movies when one of the crew members has a "bad feeling" about the bank job they are about to pull. But the wheels are already set in motion, and it's too late to turn back. They end up doing the bank job anyway, but then halfway through, they get ambushed by the cops. That's how I felt about Patrick's wedding. I knew something terrible was going to go down tonight; my spider-sense was warning me—and my spider-sense was rarely wrong.

I knew things were going to go sideways when I first saw the wedding itinerary. Especially with a three-hour gap between the end of the ceremony and the start of the dinner reception. They included that so that the room could be flipped. That's where you rearrange the room from one layout to another. Basically, reusing the space, and in this case, the room would be moved from a formal ceremony into a dinner setting. The three hours would be tight for the catering staff and me to move tables and chairs, but a lot of time to kill for guests. In my case, it meant rearranging all my DJ equipment and speakers from one side of the room to the other.

Most guests hit up the pub next door. Day drinking in the middle of the afternoon on empty stomachs never ends well.

Nothing can prepare you for nights like this. You can vet out some of the high-maintenance clients, pick a venue you know is suitable, and get an idea of how the night will go beforehand. Still, at the end of the day, sometimes bad gigs just happen. They are out of your control.

This was shaping up to be one of those nights.

"Sucks," he shouts over the music.

"Change the song," she yells at me.

"Next, bro," he looks at me, motioning to wrap up the song.

"Weaaaaaaaaaaak!" she screams.

The couple from hell was standing in front of me, critiquing every song for the past 30 minutes, being so obnoxious that I could only assume they did this at every wedding. It only takes one guest to ruin your wedding. This couple was making it unbearable.

I'm fine with a bit of criticism, but it was completely bumping! Not to mention, the songs were directly off the Groom's Must Play List. Who does this at a wedding?

I was starting to feel myself boiling up.

"Last Call is less than half an hour away. You can do this!" I tell myself, giving myself an internal much-needed pep talk.

It doesn't end. Knob Knocker and his girlfriend continue for the next 25 minutes.

"This DJ blows," he laughs toward his friends.

"WEEEEEEEEAAAAAAK bro!" she screams again in my direction.

Then there's a tap on my shoulder. The bartender is pointing at an invisible watch on his wrist while mouthing the words "Last Call." Without removing my headphones, I nod my head, give him a fist bump, and jump on the mic.

"Congrats to the bride and groom! Thanks so much, everybody, it's the Last Call at the bar!" I'm so close to getting out of here I can almost taste it. A few more songs and I never have to see this couple again.

Finally, the catering staff is turning the lights are on. I've made it!

The final throngs of guests moan at the bright Ugly Lights. Success! I snap off my headphones and turn the Master Volume on the mixer all the way down. My night is officially over.

The MC shakes my hand, "Hey buddy, can I borrow the mic for a second? I need to make an announcement." I turn up the volume on the mixer back up and pass him the wireless mic.

"Hey everybody!" he speaks into the mic. "The after-party is at the Roxy!"

The popular late-night venue downtown is cheap, open late, and filled with a nasty drunken crowd. These guys will fit in just perfectly.

Drunken hollering ensues. The crowd is divided. Some shout, "Yes!" and a few others shout, "Noooooooo, The Roxy sucks!"

I don't give a shit where you guys go. I'm out of here, I think to myself.

As the MC turns to pass the mic back to me, it's snatched from his hand. It's Knob Knocker.

"Fuck the Roxy!"

A black blur and feedback whizz through my speakers as he launches my wireless mic across the room. It smashes on the floor on the other side of the room with a thud. For a few seconds, I'm unable to register what just happened.

My brain is on fire!

Muscle memory takes over, and I instinctively leap from behind my table, run over to the microphone, and fish it up from the puddle of spilled drinks and end-of-the-night shoe grime. I'm seeing nothing but red as I shout into the mic.

"That's a FUCKING 300 dollar mic, you mother fucker!" I shout, getting my night's worth of frustration off my chest. I'm actually a little surprised that the mic still works. Unfortunately, the speakers are still on full volume.

Up until 10 seconds ago, the crowd was ready to head out the door to The Roxy. Now, it's a different ballgame. The room is deafeningly silent with all eyes on me. Oooooops. As with Hannah's Brother and Danny Voss, I really stuck my foot in it this time.

No surprise, Knob Knocker is now right in my face yelling and screaming. He's probably been waiting all night for this. The main difference between Hannah's Brother and Danny Voss is that this time I'm not intimidated.

This time I'm really fucking pissed off.

Years of being put in these situations have reached boiling point. Years of drunk ungrateful guests, being bullied, called names, and pushed around is over. I'm pissed off with the sleepless nights and missing my family every weekend. The blood, sweat, and tears that go into every gig are all for what? Jackasses like this guy and his girlfriend? Bridezillas, puke, karate chops, Aunt Martha . . .

It's all come to a head, and now I've had it. This time I'm not backing down.

"You threw my fucking mic!" I shout back in his face.

Before I know it, the entire room is gathered around us. Knob Knocker's girlfriend now starts screaming at me. It's a room full of drunken idiots versus me, the only sober one in the room.

Which side do they take? I have to be honest; it's not looking good for my case.

The groom is now standing between us, hands on our chests, keeping us separated. The insults continue to get hurled my way while Knob Knocker and his girlfriend are inches away from my face. People start pulling out their phones to document this most bizarre ending to the day.

The caterers start to push in the crowd when the bartender jumps from behind the bar. Things are spiraling out of control. It's not how I envisioned the night ending, but it's too late, just like the bank heist gone wrong. It's too far gone now . . .

No matter how frustrated a wedding DJ gets, he can't call a guest a mother fucker.

Reality kicks in.

I fucked up.

Badly.

I knew right then; this was the end of my wedding DJ career.

THE NEXT MORNING, 11:18AM.

"Ahhhhhhhh damn," I groan as soon as I turn on my phone.

I get a text from Patrick: *Call Me ASAP!*

I rehearse my defense as I dial the number; I know what's coming.

"I am very disappointed in what happened," he starts.

His voice becomes a blur. Anger and depression wash over me.

"It's only a microphone. You were very aggressive," he continues. "We felt you could have handled it so much better."

I wanted to reach through the phone and yell in his face.

Me? Aggressive? How about your Drunk-Ass-Mother-Fucking Knob Knocker loser friend and his girlfriend?

Instead, I sit in silence, taking it, listening to the other voice on the end of the phone.

I had flawlessly executed every portion of the 12-hour day, gave them an epic dance party, accommodated multiple last-minute requests for the ceremony, charmed every drunken aunt, work colleague, and friend—all for nothing.

I spend the rest of the day searching YouTube for videos for anything with titles like:

- "Wedding DJs Gone Wild"
- "Wedding DJ Goes Crazy"
- "Worst Wedding DJ Ever"

Sometimes unexpected events can end up changing your life. It happens to people every day. Things you have worked years for can end in seconds. A thrown mic and I knew my wedding DJ career was finished.

But there was one last nail in the coffin when I knew it was officially over, and this time it was completely out of my control.

. . . AND DONE

March 11th, 2020

That was the day I had my last gig in the real world.

"Did you hear Tom Hanks has coronavirus?" the guy running the Photo Booth tells me.

"Wait . . . what?" I ask, not sure I heard correctly.

"Yeah, and the NBA has shut down for the season!" he continues.

I had just finished a rocking corporate party, but little did I know that the wedding industry was going to be flipped on its head for the foreseeable future. Within days, the cancelations started to roll in. First, my April 2020 weddings canceled, then May, June, July, and August. Month after month fell like dominoes. Soon, the entire year was completely canceled, like a referee just blew a whistle on the final seconds of the game. My once full calendar was now empty.

With that came a loss of identity. I was now a DJ that wasn't able to DJ. Being a DJ wasn't just a job, it was who I was! I was DJ BFAD.

I needed the crowd and craved the energy. Even though my workplace was not typical and often toxic, I had grown to love the chaos. I both loathed it and craved it at the same time—the proverbial Stockholm Syndrome.

For the first few months of the pandemic, I was in a state of disbelief. However, I was no stranger to this feeling; it was how I felt back in July 2009 when I was fired. Everything was out of my control. It was a bitter pill to swallow, but the reality was I was now back at square one.

That summer began the familiar pattern of 2009. Late-night couch surfing and drinking way too much. A feeling of hopelessness consumed me. For so many years, I had measured success by how many weddings I did. The more days I filled in the calendar meant the more money I had. Which meant the more successful I was.

Or so I thought.

Another night spent aimlessly surfing the net, I take a swig of beer and click on a random zombie movie that popped up on my recommendations list. About halfway through, one of the heroes gets his arm chewed off by a zombie.

"Come on!" I yell at the screen. He should have survived. He killed hundreds of zombies, was an expert warrior, and had grenades and knives strapped all over his body. Instead, he gets caught out trying to save a little girl hiding behind a garbage can.

What a rip-off way to die! I think to myself while shutting off the movie. As I take another swig of beer and look for something else to watch, it dawned on me! I needed to change my mindset.

It's not about how many zombies you kill; it's about whether you survive the apocalypse.

No matter how many weddings I did in the past, I had survived 12 years. That was a feat in itself. I was no longer shackled to the weddings in my calendar. I was now free to do whatever I wanted!

It was both liberating and terrifying at the same time.

When you're pushing yourself through a moment and make it out the other side unscathed, you kind of look at yourself and say, "Fuck ya! I made it." I'm okay. I did good.

And I couldn't be happier.

EPILOGUE

A SIMPLE EXCHANGE AT THE TRAFFIC LIGHTS

Sitting at the intersection of Keefer and Main St, I drift off into a daydream waiting for the light to change.

My mind is preoccupied. I'm picking up some tacos in Gastown for a stay-at-home date night with Emma and the kids. Saturday nights at home with the family are still a novelty after 12 years of non-stop weddings.

The windows are rolled down on this warm summer night. It's the first summer in years with no planners, no timelines, and no set music cues.

"BEEEEEEE-FAAAADDDD!" a voice calls out from the car beside me.

I snap out of my daze and look over to my left and see a clean white convertible BMW. The passenger, a cool dude with shoulder-length hair, leans over the passenger seat, smiling at me. I give a nod and smile. He must see the DJ BFAD logo on the side of my car. *Another job on my "gotta get that removed" list,* I think to myself.

"You did my wedding two years ago!" the driver shouts over.

"What?" I laugh, surprised. "Where?" I shout back. I have no idea who this is.

"It's Jude! You did my wedding at Rosewood!"

I sit for a second as I flip through the mental Rolodex of hundreds of weddings stored in my memory. Finally, it clicks. I remember! The best couple, last-minute booking with some awesome vendors. It was one of those nights where everything just clicked. There was a great feeling in the air; people were happy, there was no stress, and the best music was on their playlist.

Jamiroquai, Sugarhill Gang, David Bowie, Snoop Dogg, Jay-Z, Missy Elliott, Rihanna, Destiny's Child, TLC, Calvin Harris, Prince, Whitney Houston, Run DMC, A Tribe Called Quest, Daft Punk, Robyn, MIA, Stevie Wonder, Otis Redding, Curtis Mayfield, Janet Jackson, Fatboy Slim, Pixies, New Order, The Stone Roses, Britney, Marvin Gaye, Diana Ross, Otis Redding, Funkadelic, Bob Marley, The Ramones, Rage Against The Machine, Nine Inch Nails, Fugazi . . .

It was one of those nights where I actually had a great time! It was all about the music and showing off my versatility. It definitely didn't feel like I was working. In fact, it kind of reminded me of why I started to DJ in the first place all those years ago. It took me back to 1984, listening to CKOC in the basement and making my mixtapes.

"Oh, Jude, WOW, great to see you!" I shout back. "I didn't recognize you with long hair!"

He laughs. "You were great at our wedding! Everyone still talks about you!"

"It was an awesome wedding. Thanks for having me!" I shout back. I spot two empty car seats in the back seat of the convertible.

"You and Skye have kids now?"

"Two boys, twins!" he shouts back, then gives a wave as the light turns green and the car moves forward.

"Take it easy, BFAD!"

A silly grin fills my face as I pull forward from the traffic light.

I had totally forgotten about his wedding . . . they still talk about me?

It was also the night I received my best thank you.

I found out Skye's dad had died a few weeks before the wedding from a long, drawn-out cancer battle. He desperately tried to hold on so he would be able to walk his daughter down the aisle. Before the ceremony started, the officiant mentioned this and announced, "This is not a wake, but a celebration!"

I felt an obligation to make it the best party ever. I was about as nervous as I could be before a gig. As the dancing kicked off, Skye approached the DJ booth:

"Could you get on the mic and dedicate a song to my father?" she asked.

"Of course, which song?"

"Queen 'Don't Stop Me Now.'"

As soon as I dropped the track, the dance floor was immediately wall-to-wall packed. And it didn't stop until the end of the night.

The officiant was right. It was a celebration!

When the lights came on at the end of the night, Skye came up to thank me. She had tears in her eyes and said it was more than she could have ever hoped for.

"I know my dad was here tonight."

My best thank you. More meaningful and heartfelt than any random group of guests shouting my name at the end of the night.

I snap back to reality and start to calculate the math in my head. Fifty weddings a year, 12 years, that's over 500 weddings! I wonder if many other couples look back fondly on their nights with me?

For a minute, I feel good about all those years I spent in the trenches of the wedding industry. And for the first time, I feel appreciated.

Maybe it was all worth it after all.

THE END

ABOUT THE AUTHOR

Brent Faddies (DJ BFAD) has had a passion for music ever since he received his first record player for Christmas at 8 years old. His passion for music flourished into becoming a full-time DJ from 2009–2021. Brent has performed at over 500 weddings and lives in Vancouver, BC., with his wife and two kids.

ACKNOWLEDGMENTS

I would like to thank the hundreds of wedding couples I have worked with over the years! Every single one—the good, the bad, and the ugly—I am forever grateful for the parties we rocked.

I would also like to acknowledge the absolutely stellar wedding industry in Vancouver. All the photographers, officiants, planners, videographers, venues, caterers, bartenders, wait staff, and fellow DJs. It's not always an easy gig, but you all make it worthwhile.

Infinite thanks to my wife, Emma, and my boys, Samuel and Noah.

Finally, thanks to all who supported, danced, high-fived, puked, partied, got up, fell down, spilled drinks, made requests, gave me hugs, screamed my name, told me I sucked, and gave me a reason to do what I do best.

Cover Photo: Roger Mahler Photography.

Cover Stars: (left to right) Noah, Uncle Darren, Samuel, Mat (Bored-Trash-Horsehead), Emma Planner, Ashley Bride, Graham Groom, Sally Bridesmaid, Miss Mosco Moonshine, Destiny, and James. Thanks for a super fun photo session!

Made in the USA
Las Vegas, NV
19 December 2021

38771485R00193